BAD CLOWNS

BAD CLOWNS

BENJAMIN RADFORD

UNIVERSITY OF NEW MEXICO PRESS
ALBUQUERQUE

Library of Congress Cataloging-in-Publication Data
Radford, Benjamin, 1970–
 Bad clowns / Benjamin Radford. — First edition.
     pages cm
 Includes bibliographical references and index.
 ISBN 978-0-8263-5666-6 (Paper : alk. paper) — ISBN 978-0-8263-5667-3 (Electronic)
 1. Clowns—History. I. Title.
 GV1828.R3 2016
 791.3'3—dc23
                                    2015029026

Cover illustrations: *Balloons* by Joshua Hoffine © 2015. *Phantom clowns* illustration by
    James Black.
Designed by Lila Sanchez
Composed in Adobe Caslon Pro, Helvetica Neue, and Muleshoe

For those who believed in me, and for Stéphane Charbonnier, Farkhunda Malikzada, Narendra Dabholkar, Lt. Gen. Romeo Dallaire, David Finkelhor, and Elizabeth Loftus.

Universal is the casting of the antagonist, the representative of evil, in the role of the clown. Devils—both the lusty thickheads and the sharp, clever deceivers—are always clowns.

—JOSEPH CAMPBELL, *The Hero with a Thousand Faces*

Contents

Acknowledgments

I am grateful for the support and assistance of many people, including John Boyd, Lori Cuthbert, Paul Heltzel, Jonathan, Marce, Julia Lavarnway, Eliza Sutton, Shana Pedroncelli, Celestia Ward, the staff at Satellite Coffee in Corrales who provided a place for caffeine-fueled hard-copy edits, and especially the Inner Sanctum Irregulars. Special thanks to Nat Glick and Coriander Pyle for inspiration.

Introduction

W hy a book about bad clowns?

Perhaps a better question is "Why *not* a book about bad clowns?" They are all around us: on television, in movies, video games, books, and elsewhere. Bad clowns have—much to the irritation of good clowns—over the years become the most recognizable type of clown. Yet there is relatively little (even semiserious) scholarship about these villainous vagabonds.

This book goes far beyond trotting out the familiar bad clown tropes of John Wayne Gacy and Pennywise. They are included here, of course, but you'll also find bizarre, lesser-known stories of weird clown antics including S&M clowns; Ronald McDonald protests; Bozo obscenity; clowns in vans abducting children; evil-clown scares in Europe and North America; backstage scenes at Marvel Comics with Obnoxio the Clown; Crotchy, the clown who forced the Nebraska Supreme Court to watch him masturbate; dip clowns; troll clowns; and much more.

I myself harbor no particular love nor fear or hatred of clowns, whether bad or good; this book is not an attempt to exorcise demons or resolve some latent childhood phobia. It is instead a mostly serious blend of academic scholarship, pop culture critique, folklore and urban legend research, psychology, and sociological analysis. I wanted to look at variations of the bad clown theme to understand a phenomenon, just as

I did in my 2011 book *Tracking the Chupacabra: The Vampire Beast in Fact, Fiction, and Folklore.* Bad clowns and chupacabras have more in common than may appear at first glance: they are both mysterious and scary.

I struggled with what to title this book. Titles are often tricky, but this one was devilishly difficult. *Evil Clowns* was too limiting; while many clowns in this parade of greasepainted malcontents are indeed evil, I wanted to peek behind the tent of the dark circus to explore shades of clown corruption. *Bad*, then, includes not merely malicious intent but exhibiting boorish, mean-spirited, unpleasant, disagreeable, and insulting behavior. It's the clown you fear will appear at your birthday party—or over your bed as you sleep. There are countless bad clowns that could be included here; my goal is not to provide a comprehensive listing of all of them (an exhausting effort for me, resulting in an unenlightening read for you), but instead to sample the variety of the discomfort that clowns have wreaked on the earth.

It's difficult to assign a specific cultural meaning to the bad clown because it is such a malleable archetype. Like any other symbol, the evil clown—unlike the default, ordinary, "good" clown whose meaning is fairly fixed over time as playful, whimsical, and friendly—can be adopted or adapted to mean whatever one wants it to mean, and varies by context. As a trickster symbol the bad clown may represent trickery, deceit, death, malevolence, mischief, chaos, evil, betrayal, humor, power, rebellion, defiance of authority, wisdom, and so on. Though the bad clown archetype is a popular one in America and around the world, it is rarely celebrated in its generic form; instead, specific, distinctive bad clowns capture the public's imagination and percolate through pop culture. Dozens are discussed in this book, from Bozo to Pennywise. The most famous bad clown in the world is the DC Comics supervillain the Joker, and thus he appears often.

The clown has played an important role in all societies and cultures, and the bad clown is an inherent part of that. You can no more separate a good clown from a bad clown than a clown from his shadow. This is not to say that all clowns are evil, of course—though I was told that was the case in earnest several times while researching this book—but instead that because clowns are human (or at least have human attributes) they have good and bad sides. It is another side of the same coin; if you keep

FIGURE I.I. *Bizarro* © 2006 Dan Piraro, distributed by King Features. Reprinted by permission.

a quarter faceup on your desk or shelf, it will always remain faceup every time you glance at it. But another, hidden side is there if you choose to look.

Offering an overarching monolithic cultural meaning to the bad clown is a fool's errand. The folkloric and cultural literature on the trickster archetype is vast and varied, and it is thus far beyond the scope of this book. There are as many nuanced meanings to bad clowns as there are fans of bad clowns. Many are attracted by the ironic, contradictory juxtaposition of the bad clown; for others it's the appeal of the suave bad boy.

Not everyone who dresses like a clown actually *is* a clown, and thus the definition of *clown* throughout this book is necessarily broad. For example reputed Chicago Outfit mafia boss and racketeer Joey Lombardo is nicknamed "Joey the Clown," though he got the appellation not because of any actual clown antics or costume but because of his playful and defiant nature (such as grinning for police mug shots). Many of the most evil and best-known clowns are not professional clowns at all, such as the Joker and John Wayne Gacy. Real clowns—those who make a career out of delighting children and adults in circuses, at parties, and elsewhere—are barely represented here. Only a dozen or so professional clowns have been accused of serious crimes or evil acts, a vanishingly small number in proportion to the number of clowns around the world. Statistically you'd be more likely to win the lottery than to encounter an evil person who also happens to be a clown. Caveats aside, I don't expect this book to be appreciated by professional clowns, who understandably resent the bad clown stereotype and wish it would just go away.[1]

But ignoring bad clowns won't make them disappear, and like it or not the bad one is the clown we love to hate. From Foo Foo to Frenchy, Punch to Pennywise, Shakes to Sweet Tooth, a seemingly inexhaustible supply of bad clowns keeps coming, bursting out of a tiny car into the media, each more vile than the last. Bad clowns exist mostly in our imaginations as vigilante antiheroes of the id. These clowns are gleefully beyond redemption: cruel and comical, vituperative and violent, uncouth and (sometimes) unclothed.

They are bad clowns, and this is their story.

CHAPTER I

A Short History of the Earliest Clowns

Clowns have been around in one form or another for millennia; they constitute an ancient archetype encompassing countless variations. In her classic study *The Fool: His Social and Literary History*, Enid Welsford traces the clown (more specifically, the European clown) to

> ancient Greece, where we discover him [in various forms]; now as a squat slave with padded stomach, pelting the spectators with nuts or parodying the wanton orgies of Dionysus, now as a bald-headed, ass-eared, hook-nosed fellow bearing a striking resemblance to the half-witted jesters of a later period. This bald-headed clown or *sannio* was a long-lived gentleman, for we find him still flourishing in the early years of the Roman Empire as "secondary mime" or "stupidus" whose business it was to repeat the words and make unsuccessful attempts to imitate the actions of others, and to be deceived by everybody. He wore a long pointed hat, a multicoloured patchwork dress, and according to St. Chrysostom it was part of his duty to "be slapped at the public expense." (Welsford 1966, 278)

This theme of slapping clowns for amusement and pleasure would carry over into later plays and films such as *He Who Gets Slapped*.

Clown historian Beryl Hugill notes that "the actual word 'clown' did not enter the language until the sixteenth century. It is of Low German origin and means a countryman or peasant. Its original meaning is allied in sense to the word for a Dutch or German farmer, 'boor,' from which we get the adjective 'boorish'. So 'clown' meant someone who was doltish or ill-bred" (Hugill 1980, 14). The everyman nature of the clown was established early, and the figure came and went over the centuries but flourished during the Renaissance in the commedia dell'arte, a theater genre popular in Italy in the sixteenth century.

> The characters of the commedia dell'arte were caricatures of familiar types representing young and old, urban and rural, sophisticated and rustic, rich and poor, and native and foreigner. These types were divided into high and low characters. The former included lovers who were young and attractive and whose speech was the cultivated, courtly dialect of Tuscany. Low characters included clowns (*zanni*) and their female counterparts, the maids. . . . Harlequin, Brighella, Pierrot (Pedrolino), and Pulcinella are all low, masked clowns. . . . Harlequin and Brighella . . . were both from Bergamo, a town considered by Venetians to be both rustic and crude. Harlequin was the more crude of the two—always hungry, always nosy, always getting into trouble, and always vexing his master. His costume was made up of multicolored patches and a wooden sword or bat hung at his side (the original slapstick). He wore a black half-mask with bushy eyebrows and mustache, carbuncles, and a snub nose, above which he wore a felt hat with a rabbit's tail. (Royce 1998, 135–36)

The crude, chaotic Harlequin character (typically wearing a mask and a colorful, diamond-patterned costume) is clearly a clown, but his roots run sinister, as there is a link between him and the diabolical world: "Harlequin appears first in history or legend as an aerial spectre or demon, leading the ghostly nocturnal cortege known as the Wild Hunt. [Eventually] the Hunt lost some of its terrors and the wailing procession of lost souls turned into a troupe of comic demons who flew merrily

FIGURE 1.1. *Harlequin* (1888–1890), by Paul Cezanne. National Gallery of Art, Washington, DC. Photograph by Alexander R. Pruss, used by permission of a Creative Commons license, Wikimedia Commons.

through the air to the sound of song and tinkling bells" (Welsford 1966, 292). Indeed, the Harlequin character often appeared in plays and stories as involved with magical creatures including fairies (which, despite the sanitized and Disneyfied depictions most modern children are familiar with, can be evil, cruel creatures; for an excellent discussion of fairy sadism and "intrafairy violence and warfare," see Silver 1999).

> In the next century the Roman du Fauvel shows a further comic and dramatic development of the "maisinie Harlequin," which now appears not as a band of aerial sprites, but as a noisy troupe of mummers, rioting outside the bridal chamber of a newly married couple whom they desire to mock. The diabolical aspect of Harlequin was not, however, wholly forgotten. . . . It was mainly through the religious drama that Harlequin developed from an aerial demon into a comic devil, and so was prepared for his final migration to the Italian comic stage. For Harlequin has a mixed ancestry, and is himself an odd hybrid creature, in part a devil created by popular fancy, in part a wandering mountebank from Italy. (Welsford 1966, 292–93)

Though the echoes of this diabolical, itinerant trickster can be seen in modern clowns, written accounts of his exploits are at least four centuries old:

> Harlequin the Clown makes his first appearance in literature in two curious poems published in Paris in 1585 . . . where he is represented as a kind of diabolical acrobat. . . . One poem . . . relates how one night Harlequin had a vision of Mother Cardine, a villainous old woman who in her lifetime kept a brothel in Paris, and had now risen from the underworld in order to beg "her son" to deliver her from the torments of Hell. As soon as he awoke from the dream Harlequin journeyed to the river of death, leapt onto Charon's shoulders as lightly as a monkey, and proceeded to divert that grim ferryman by putting out his tongue, rolling his eyes and performing a thousand antics. Having made a further conquest of [three-headed dog] Cerberus, he went on to divert even the King of the Underworld by his acrobatic feats.

Harlequin's comic persuasion worked, and in return he was promised anything he desired—whereupon he promptly requested that Mother Cardine be restored to life, and his mission was accomplished (Welsford 1966, 294). The clown-defeats-Death theme would reappear a century later in the Punch and Judy show (see next chapter).

Harlequin, for much of his existence, was silent. Like most clowns he performed in pantomime. This silence is one aspect that makes a clown mysterious and unnerving, for his thoughts and motivations—whether benevolent or malicious—may be on his mind but are not on his tongue. (The quiet-killer theme is also exploited in modern horror and slasher films, with silent masked murderers such as Michael Myers and Jason Voorhees relentlessly stalking their helpless prey.) Some later incarnations of the Harlequin employed speech, but today most clowns (such as those in circuses) don't speak—not as a scare tactic but simply as a practical matter. A traveling circus may visit dozens of countries, and a clown can perform anywhere since their silent slapstick and pratfalls are universal and need no translation. Some clowns, such as North American ones who perform at birthday parties, of course, often speak and tell jokes.

It's interesting to note that historically the clown figure is generally devoid of allegiance; he has no masters and is a man in full and at his own command. Enid Welsford discusses a character in the play *Life Is a Dream*, in which a clown, Clarin, is caught in a war between powerful foes. He says,

> To me it matters not a pin,
> Which doth lose or which doth win,
> If I can keep out of the way!—
> So aside here I will go,
> Acting like a prudent hero,
> Even as the Emperor Nero
> Took things coolly long ago.
> Or if care I cannot shun,
> Let it 'bout mine ownself be;
> Yes, here hidden I can see
> All the fighting and the fun
> (Quoted in Welsford 1966, 280).

Clarin is a capricious clown looking after his own self-interest and perfectly happy to toady up to whoever wins the battle.

Certainly some clowns were employed by circuses or were jesters kept at the pleasure of a royal court, and to that extent they had some allegiance to those who fed and housed them. But even then they would often mock those they served; a jester might gently (and safely) rib a king about his weight or wealth, for example, while a circus clown might make a joke about how expensive the cotton candy sold at the concession stand is. "The court jester was a fool licensed to speak his mind only in the disguise of nonsense," notes Hugill. "This tolerance stemmed from the belief that idiots were divine and that their presence formed a magic protection from evil. Consequently, royal households generally included an imbecile, for entertainment as well as protection" (Hugill 1980, 14). This theme of the clown role serving as a protected pretext for expressing truth or unpopular opinion would become an important part of later clowns.

The *commedia dell'arte* was popular for centuries and can still be found today; its spawn Harlequin, however, is more of a relic. As times changed the clown shed old clothes for a newer form. In his examination "Clowns on the Verge of a Nervous Breakdown," Andrew McConnell Stott notes that "at the end of the nineteenth century, a new figure emerged from the ashes of the harlequinade—a clown intent not on laughter but on awful, bloody revenge. He made his first appearance in Ruggerio Leoncavallo's opera *I Pagliacci* (1892). . . . Having discovered that his wife Nedda is conducting an affair, Canio, dressed for his role as a clown, confronts her and her lover and murders them both" (Stott 2012, 3).

Stott gives several examples in the decades after *I Pagliacci*, including "the anti-hero of Leonid Andreyev's absurdist play *He Who Gets Slapped* (1914), a cuckolded and plagiarized writer who becomes a circus clown to indulge his feelings of humiliation, before falling in love with, and ultimately murdering, a beautiful bareback rider; the clown who commits suicide in front of a laughing audience in Fritz Lang's *Spies* (1928); and the clown in the Lon Chaney movie *Laugh, Clown, Laugh* (1928), who, while undergoing treatment for a depression brought on by unrequited love, kills himself in the throes of an hallucination by zipping down a high wire on his head" (Stott 2012, 4). These and other films are discussed in a later chapter, and there are other threads we could follow, other early versions and variations of clowns. We briefly reviewed elements of the darker side of clown history, though there is another important historical bad clown, one so notorious and influential that he merits his own chapter. His name is Mr. Punch.

CHAPTER 2

The Despicable Rogue
Mr. Punch

No discussion of bad clowns would be complete without a certain red-capped, hook-nosed, gleeful, wife-abusing serial killer named Mr. Punch. Punch is a thoroughly despicable and remorseless thug, and indeed therein lies much of his appeal to generations of children and adults. As horror novelist Clive Barker noted, "Fools obsess me, and always have, clowns too. Punch has always fascinated me because he's so cruel and so funny at the same time" (Barker 1997, 88). He is the star in the classic Punch and Judy shows, the English version of which dates back to a performance in London's Covent Garden on May 9, 1662, marking over three and a half centuries of this peculiar play.

"And what a play it is!" exclaimed pioneering American puppeteer Tony Sarg in his 1929 foreword to *Punch and Judy: A Short History with the Original Dialogue.*

What an unexampled category of crime! Mr. Punch himself, that braggart, blusterer, wife-beater, strutting Don Juan, with a half-dozen murders to his credit, what a very prince of villains he is! Truly, children were fed upon strong meat in the days that were. In these anemic times, the career of this arch-scoundrel of the puppet-stage strikes a full and robust note. Those were the days when rogues were rogues; and when children, untroubled by

FIGURE 2.1. Portrait of Mr. Punch, based on George Cruikshank's illustration in *Punch and Judy: A Short History with the Original Dialogue* (1828).

educational theories or parental scruples, were permitted to rejoice naturally in the cracking of heads, the din of battle, the triumph of Unworthiness over Virtue and the Law. (quoted in Collier 1929, 1)

Marina Warner, in her book *Monsters of Our Own Making: The Peculiar Pleasures of Fear*, touches on a key ingredient of Mr. Punch's appeal in the play:

One of the most profound and puzzling features of the bogeyman is his seductive power: he can charm at the same time as he repels. . . . In the course of the play, Punch gleefully lays about him in a series of violent assaults. His victims include his own baby—whose torments raise the shrillest squealing from the audience. Mr. Punch is left to baby-sit by [his wife] Judy (also the butt of his big stick), and when he fails to put the baby to sleep, he batters it. Punch and Judy is considered good family fun. . . . His abuse is the play's only running gag, now and then punctuated by the puppeteer's up-to-date jokes inspired by the week's news and television. Children find it very funny.

After the death of his "babby," the ugly, obstinate, brutal gnome overcomes all obstacles—the policeman, a crocodile, a thief—which culminate in Mr. Death himself, whom Punch tempts to place his head in his own noose. (Warner 2007, 167)

FIGURE 2.2. Mr. Punch throws his crying "baby" out the window and into the audience. Illustration by George Cruikshank in *Punch and Judy: A Short History with the Original Dialogue* (1828).

The running commentary and jokes provided by the professor—the traditional name for a Punch and Judy puppeteer—are an important framing device that encourages the children to ridicule the characters. Without this context the Punch and Judy show would be an unfunny, brutal affair indeed.

Unlike the oft-silent Harlequin, Mr. Punch speaks, though with a distinctive harsh rasp created by the professor using a small mouth-held device called a swazzle. One of Punch's favorite phrases is a triumphant and demonstrative shriek—"*That's* the way to do it!"—as he deals the fatal blow with a slapstick or bat to a helpless character's body. To be fair, in the Punch and Judy show several of the characters are not passive, innocent bystanders, but give as good as they get in the abuse department—at least until Punch finally gets the upper hand.

Though there is a basic template for the Punch and Judy show, countless variations have been performed over the centuries, depending on many factors, including the social and political climate of the performance and the quality of the professor. Some shows are done against a simple black backdrop, while others employ a series of painted backgrounds that are dropped down in sequence as the scene changes from Punch's home, to the court where he's sentenced, to the gallows, and so on.

Neil Gaiman told a story about Mr. Punch in his 1994 graphic novel

The Comical Tragedy or Tragical Comedy of Mr. Punch, from DC Comics. In the story a professor explains the roles of some of the secondary characters to the narrator, a young boy. The doctor, for example, "finds Mister Punch laying on the ground. 'Are ye dead?' says he. 'Stone cold dead,' says Mister Punch, but he's lying a-course. 'I'll give you physic,' says the doctor—that's medicine the way we used to call it in the dawn days. And he comes back with his stick." "Physic, physic, physic," he says as he beats Punch. The Devil, the professor explains, "comes on at the end, to drag Mister Punch away to hell. I remember some busybodies, in the last queen's day, telling me that he ought to succeed. But he never does. There's always a Devil in the story of Mister Punch, although sometimes he's hard to find." In the story the professor offers one theory about the origin of the skeleton character in the play: "Some people says it's Judy's ghost, but I don't know. I don't know whose ghost it is haunts Mr. Punch" (Gaiman and McKean 1994, np).

Punchy History

As noted in the previous chapter, an early version of Punch, Pulcinella, appeared as a clown character in the commedia dell'arte. The plays—typically improvised sketches performed by independent actors instead of those formally employed by a theater—used a variety of stock characters, some of them wearing caricatured masks. The commedias dell'arte, along with Italian puppet shows, were seen throughout Europe for centuries, and Punch was one of their most popular characters.

Punch's exact origin is uncertain, although

an old Neapolitan legend . . . says that in vintage time a company of strolling players came to Acerra, near Naples, Italy, when the country folk were celebrating the grape harvest, and were so taken with the comical appearance and rustic wit of one of the grape-gatherers, the village hump-back, a fellow with a huge nose, whose name was Puccio d'Aniello, that they persuaded him to join their company. This Puccio d'Aniello became a great favourite, for nobody could keep from laughing at his antics; and when he died, another actor put on a false nose and a hump on his back and took, also, the name

Puccio d'Aniello—a name which, in time, became slurred by soft Italian voices into "Pulcinella." (Collier 1929, xiii)

The fact that a hunchback is offered as an inspiration for Punch is significant; in fact some researchers have suggested that Punch may be a sort of symbolic cultural caricature of a man suffering from a disease called acromegaly, which can cause exaggerated facial features, such as an enlarged chin and nose.

Like many clowns, Punch's reach was widespread. "During the Middle Ages Punch enjoyed great liberty of action, appearing in religious drama, political satire, and even opera; entertaining the company at noblemen's palaces—in many of which were well-equipped puppet stages—as well as in his humbler function as actor in a travelling marionette troupe, playing on the streets, or as chief attraction at the fairs" (Collier 1929, xiv). In his early days Punch was one of several in the puppet cast of characters (Pantaloon and Harlequin among them), though Punch, egotistical tyrant that he is, cast the others away here and there until the Comical Tragedy—or the Tragical Comedy—soon had only Mr. Punch as the star.

The comic clown became iconic and was soon widely imitated, spawning dozens of actors—and eventually marionettes and finally hand puppets—with Punch's signature twisted physiognomy and even more twisted temperament. Linda Rodriguez McRobbie, writing in *Smithsonian* magazine, notes that "Punch and Judy soon became a staple of country fair entertainment, where they would have made both adults and children laugh. As England moved to a more industrial economy, the Punch and Judy show became street fare, losing the marionette strings and picking up the recognizable red-and-white-striped booths set up in market squares or later on boardwalks and beaches at the seaside. The show could now be performed by one person using two hand puppets: Mr. Punch and whomever he was punching at the time" (McRobbie 2013a).

Though Punch is Italian, "Britain may be where Mr. Punch found fame, [and] he's beaten his wife in every country the British ever colonized. . . . One of the first puppet shows performed in America was *A Merry Dialogue Between Punch and Joan, his wife*, in Philadelphia in 1742;

OLD LONDON - Punch & Judy   COLLECTORCARD ©   C1406
                                             Croydon CR0 1HW 1973

FIGURE 2.3. An early 1970s Punch and Judy show performed in London.
Postcard from the author's collection.

George Washington, according to his accounting books, purchased tickets to see a Punch show; and Harry Houdini even did a Punch show
during his early years as a magician with a traveling circus" (McRobbie
2013a).

"That's the Way to Do It!" Or, Punch Unbowed

As would any infanticidal serial-killing clown worth his salt, Mr. Punch
has raised the ire of concerned parents for centuries. Indeed, a filmed,
realistic version of a Punch and Judy show today would likely merit a
NC-17 rating from the Motion Picture Association of America.[1] Given
the perpetual hand-wringing about the evil influences of entertainment
media on children, it's not surprising that Punch has had more than a
few scrapes with guardians of the public morals. In fact, "in 1947,
the Middlesex County Council in England banned Punch and Judy
from schools, prompting wide outcry from Punch fans and his eventual
reinstatement. More than 50 years later, in 1999 and 2000, other councils

in Britain considered banning Punch and Judy shows on the claim that they were too violent for children; they didn't, but it was close" (McRobbie 2013a).

As we have seen with clowns being given implicit and explicit license for bad behavior, the same is true of Punch: "When the English Puritans waged a bitter war against the degenerate drama of their time, they ignored the offenses of Mr. Punch, and when the German church placed a ban on the stage and all players were classed as vagabonds and law-breakers, the puppets were considered beneath the notice of the religious authorities. So the wooden Thespians seized the playhouses and took the place of the outcast actors" (Collier 1929, xv).

Part of Punch's appeal lies in his hyperbolic everyman reaction to common abuses we can all relate to: crying babies, bumbling police and authority figures, and so on. Indeed, "the structure of the drama follows the traditional shape of ritual combat, and Punch's sequential victories can be read as affirming the inextinguishable vigor of Everyman against all comers, including Death" (Warner 2007, 167). Punch ends up tossing his infernally screaming baby out the window in a move none can condone but surely all can understand. After the second hour of enduring a screaming child (summoning an apparently inexhaustible reservoir of energy) three feet away on an airplane flight, few of us could deny that tossing the little screamer out of the plane—possibly with a tiny parachute, no need to be cruel—in a Punchian move would be a reasonable remedy for all involved (including the hapless parents).

Punch's interaction with the doctor, in particular, hits home with most people. Punch may be the villain, but he is driven to such measures by a doctor who nearly matches his own cruelty. Consider this exchange between Punch and the doctor found in *Punch and Judy: A Short History with the Original Dialogue*:

Doctor: "Physic, Mr. Punch. [Hits him.] Physic for your hurt."
Punch: "Me no like physic: it give me one headache."
Doctor: "That's because you do not take enough of it. [Hits him again.] The more you take, the more good it will do you." [Hits him.]
Punch: "So you doctors always say. Try how you like it yourself."

Doctor: "We never take our own physic, if we can help it. [Hits
     him.] A little more, Mr. Punch, and you will soon be well."
     [Hits him again.]

Punch: "Oh, Doctor! Doctor! No more, no more, enough physic for
     me! I am quite well now."

Doctor: "Only another dose." [Hits him.]

Punch: "No more! Turn and turn about all is fair, you know. [Punch
     wrests the stick from the doctor and sets about giving a fatal
     beating with a dose of his own medicine.] Now, Doctor, *your
     turn* to be physicked!"

The theme of a sadistic doctor with the bedside manner of Jack the
Ripper, the compassion of a rabid Cerberus, and the saccharine, dubious
sanity of Patch Adams is hardly new. Doctors poke us, prod us, encourage
us to undergo unpleasant, painful, and sometimes even scary experiences
based on their glib assurance that it's for our own good. Surgeons cut
open our bodies, promising to rearrange our innards and leave all the
good bits intact and working better than before; doctors give us pills to
treat disease, dutifully offering hollow apologies before the onset of the
miserable side effects they've read about but don't themselves endure.
Each cut and injection and pill is a tiny metaphorical violation of our
bodies and our autonomous dignity, and though we know it's for our own
good, on some level we resent both it and the doctors who treat us. Once
again we see a clown (even one as evil as Punch) deriving much of his
support and approval from the public by acting out in ways most of us
would not dare.[2]

A fuller discussion of Punch—not to mention the Punch and Judy
show itself—is beyond the scope here; suffice it to note that Punch has
become an important part of English literature. Indeed, "Mr. Punch's
influence on British culture is unparalleled. In 2006, the Punch and Judy
show was named one of twelve icons of Englishness by the British government's Department for Culture, Media and Sport—right up there
with a cup of tea and the double-decker bus. To celebrate his 350th birthday in 2012, Mr. Punch was treated to an entire year of parties and was
the focus of a six-month-long exhibition about him at the venerable
Victoria & Albert Museum of Childhood" (McRobbie 2013a). Punch

also inspired one of England's longest-lived and most influential humor magazines, *Punch*, which began in 1841 and published through 2002; its first issue featured an engraving of Punch hanging the Devil. Punch has appeared in many venues—for example, in the 1994 British horror-comedy *Funny Man*.

We close here with one man's fond reminiscence (Collier 1929, xvii) of seeing his first Punch and Judy show as a child in the late 1800s:

There he strutted, Punch the immortal, untarnished, unchanged. There he crowed his braggart songs, wielded his club, thwacked heads royally, murdered his wife and child and the policeman, and threw them out of the window; and there he hanged the hangman with the noose intended for his own neck, and beat the Devil to death with his cudgel. "Huzzah! Huzzah! The Devil is dead!" A deliciously unregenerate ending, a veritable triumph of roguery! . . . Punch was Punch—bad as they make 'em. And how they loved him throughout the centuries!

From the original Punch and Judy dialogue as reported by John Payne Collier in his classic book *Punch and Judy: A Short History with the Original Dialogue*, when Mr. Punch is given his crying baby:

What is the matter with it. Poor thing. It has got a stomach-ache, I dare say. [Child cries.] Hush-a-bye, hush-a-bye! [Sitting down, and rolling it on his knees.] Naughty child!—Judy! [Calling.] The child has a stomach ache! Phew! Nasty child! Judy, I say! [Child continues to cry.] Keep quiet, can't you? [Boxes its ear.] Oh, you filthy child! What have you done? I won't keep such a nasty child. Hold your tongue! [Strikes the child's head several times against the side of the stage.] There! [Thwack!] There! [Thwack!] There! [Thwack!] How do you like that? I thought I stop your squalling. Get along with you, you nasty, naughty, crying child. [Throws it over the front of the stage among the spectators.] Hee, hee hee! [Laughing and singing: "Get away nasty baby; There it goes over; Thy momma's a gaby; Thy daddy's a rover."]

CHAPTER 3

The Unnatural Nature of the Evil Clown

I t's misleading to ask when clowns turned bad, for they were never really good. As our cursory review of early clown history reveals, a dark side had always lurked just below their caricatured features and painted smiles. Clowns and jesters have always been strikingly ambiguous characters, neither clear heroes nor villains, but either or both at different times as suits their murky purposes. The evil clown character may have flourished and found new fame over the past few decades, but there is nothing new about it. Joseph Campbell, in his classic, *The Hero with a Thousand Faces*, notes that in mythology the clown and evil are inextricably linked: "Universal too is the casting of the antagonist, the representative of evil, in the role of the clown. Devils—both the lusty thickheads and the sharp, clever deceivers—are always clowns. . . . They are the mistakers of shadow for substance: they symbolize the inevitable imperfections of the realm of shadow, and so long as we remain this side of the veil cannot be done away" (Campbell 1972, 294).

The bad clown is a compelling character and has inspired many people (of varying degrees of ability and creativity) in many media. From comic books to cartoons, video games to films, bad clowns have made an indelible mark on popular culture. There seems to be no pathology too sick, no act too depraved, that a bad clown won't gleefully take on to please his (or, less often, her) adoring fans.

Clowns may be scary to many people, but they are not inherently threatening the way a coiled rattlesnake or knife-wielding mugger is. The fear of clowns stems from a latent, *potential* harm, a suspicion that the seemingly silly and harmless pratfalling fool before us may in fact not be so silly, so foolish, or so harmless. Most of us (the adults anyway) understand that the clown is an act—a fake and fantastical persona adopted for a short time as part of a social event. It can be cute and funny at the time, though we may not want to be around when he decides to stop acting.

Carlo Rotella, writing in *American Scholar*, described a childhood friend obsessed with clowns:

> Tom C. cultivated a morbid obsession with clowns. Instead of merely doodling in class, he created obsessive dossiers of clown types: the savage Jester, the crocodile-teared Sad Clown, the enigmatic Bowler Hat, the rare Plume Clown, the annihilating Whiteface. He practiced different stylized ways of saying the word *clown*—drawing it out, barking it sharply, stretching his rubbery features to make a demented face while he said it, adopting a strangled or booming voice—as if he could figure out what was hiding in the word by turning it inside out. . . . Tom trained himself to wake up in the night and tape-record descriptions of his clown-filled dreams while they were fresh in his mind, and he kept his dream tape in the 'Freak Out Box,' but one day he decided that listening to the tape might do him irreparable harm, so he destroyed it without ever playing it. (Rotella 2004, 52)

What is the nature of a clown that makes it scary? "The great silent horror actor Lon Chaney Sr. once said, 'A clown is funny in the circus ring, but what would be the normal reaction to opening a door at midnight and finding the same clown there in the moonlight?" (Barker 1997, 88). As for clowns and devils in the moonlight, Jack Nicholson's Joker asks the widely quoted question, "Tell me, my friend, have you ever danced with the devil in the pale moonlight?" in the 1989 film *Batman*. Clive Barker, in his BBC series and book *A-Z of Horror*, notes that "Robert Bloch, the author of *Psycho*, agreed with Chaney: 'That, to me, is the essence of true horror—

the clown, at midnight. Horror is something peculiar to the individual—a small child's (and frequently an adult's) fear of the dark . . . and most particularly the phantoms of the imagination that populate the dark. The fear of a human being who doesn't act, think, or look like a human being'" (Barker 1997, 88). Comedian Bobcat Goldthwait has offered his own take on why clowns are scary: "Most people get nervous when they see a clown, because clowns give off this vibe that they are going to make you touch their penis" (quoted in Stott 2012, 5).

Books about circuses feature many clowns, and though most of them are funny, silly, and playful, it's not difficult to find genuinely (and unintentionally) frightening ones. Everything about clowns is exaggerated, from their primary-color clothing palette to their props (see figure 3.1). They wear shoes and eyeglasses many times too big and may accentuate their thin necks by wearing collars several sizes too large. The exaggeration almost always extends toward the greater extremes for the simple reason that they mostly perform in front of crowds, who need to see and hear their props. A tiny pair of eyeglasses or a miniscule ear trumpet may, in theory, be just as funny as gigantic ones, but these will be lost on anyone more than a few feet away. For this reason clowns rarely deal in subtlety and nuance; instead they are creatures of the large and the loud, often armed with denuded dead latex fowl.

Some clowns paint eyes on their eyelids, giving the unnerving illusion that their eyes are always open, always watching. Clown Felix Adler appeared on the May 1950 cover of *Buick* magazine with a mouth painted on his chin, giving the appearance of a gaping, sparsely toothed maw just below his real mouth—creepy enough, until of course he opens his mouth and suddenly seems to have two open mouths on his face, one atop the other. This seemingly genial face paint could easily inspire a character in a Stephen King or Clive Barker novel.

We typically see clowns interacting with others, usually other clowns. As an observer we understand the situation and are comfortable with it. But if there is no one else around—no other clowns or volunteers from the audience (and they are always volunteers) to act as the clown's foil—then by implication we are suddenly Shanghaied into the situation and onto their ship of fools. As Lon Chaney noted, as long as there is a third person for the clown to interact with, we feel safe, but if alone with a clown we are nonconsensually part of the act, for better or worse (and, we often suspect, worse). Monty Python veteran Eric Idle mused on the fear that clowns bring: "Clowns are grotesquely painted, horrifying mad people who come lurching toward us, threatening us, involving us" (quoted in Weinberg 2007, 37).

FIGURE 3.1. Implements of comic destruction used by circus clowns, including guns, explosives, and giant mallets on display at the Ringling Museum. Photo by the author.

FIGURE 3.2. Clown shoes on display at the Ringling Museum. Photo by the author.

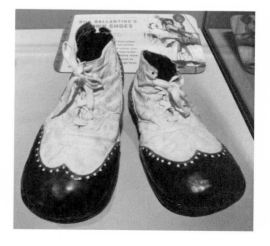

Janus the Clown: Laughter and Sadness, Horror and Humor

The tension and fear inherent in many bad clowns derives from the contradiction and contrast between a depressed, psychotic man being forced to adopt a persona of a happy, wacky character he clearly is not. Strange actions that would otherwise be noticed (or even draw psychiatric scrutiny) are assumed—at first anyway—to simply be part of a clown's bizarre repertoire.

This idea of a scary Jekyll-and-Hyde clown can be traced in part to Charles Dickens, according to author Andrew McConnell Stott, an English professor at the University of Buffalo. Dickens edited the memoir of famed British clown Joseph Grimaldi (1778–1837). Grimaldi was a troubled man, his life peppered with real-life tragedy ranging from physical disability to the death of his wife during childbirth. Stott notes that Grimaldi "was subject to debilitating bouts of depression when not on stage. . . . Over the course of his career, the striking contrast between Grimaldi's private melancholy and his ability to create public laughter came to be seen as the key to his talent, a contrast made largely possible by the emphatic difference between his appearance both in and out of makeup" (Stott 2012, 9). Grimaldi was one of the best-known clowns of his day and hugely influential to clowning. His act was widely imitated and the idea that a touch of madness (or tragedy) was needed to spark his genius was part of the ideological baggage and became inseparable from his routines.

Smithsonian magazine writer Linda Rodriguez McRobbie explains Dickens's role in creating and perpetuating the scary clown:

> After Grimaldi died penniless and an alcoholic in 1837 . . . Dickens was charged with editing Grimaldi's memoirs. Dickens had already hit upon the dissipated, drunken clown theme in his 1836 *The Pickwick Papers*. In the serialized novel, he describes an off-duty clown—reportedly inspired by Grimaldi's son—whose inebriation and ghastly, wasted body contrasted with his white face paint and clown costume. Unsurprisingly, Dickens's version of Grimaldi's life was, well, Dickensian, and, Stott says, imposed a "strict economy": For every laugh he wrought from his audiences, Grimaldi suffered commensurate pain.

Stott credits Dickens with watering the seeds in popular imagination of the scary clown—he'd even go so far as to say Dickens *invented* the scary clown—by creating a figure who is literally destroying himself to make his audiences laugh. What Dickens did was to make it difficult to look at a clown without wondering what was going on underneath the make-up: Says Stott, "It becomes impossible to disassociate the character from the actor." That Dickens's version of Grimaldi's memoirs was massively popular meant that this perception, of something dark and troubled masked by humor, would stick. (McRobbie 2013b)

Thus, in this view, much of the unease with clowns stems from the real or imagined contradiction between the public and private personas of the clown. Tony Timpone, longtime editor of the horror film–themed *Fangoria* magazine, has a similar view: "I think what makes a clown scary to some people is that this happy-go-lucky face could be hiding something. You don't really know what's underneath the phony face—it could be a psychopath, so it's really disturbing. A lot of clown faces, it's almost like a forced or exaggerated sense of happiness, or innocence perhaps, that can be very threatening in the wrong circumstances."

If a clown's greasepainted smile can vanish with the wipe of a dirty rag, then for all we know the man behind the mask could be very different: "The popular image of clowns and clown performers tend to be lonely guys, crying on the inside type, who try to bring happiness to the world, but in their own lives they're very unhappy. A lot of actors and comedians known for being clowns tend to be very unhappy. I think of Peter Sellers, his personal life was a mess, and a lot of the big buffoonish characters like John Candy and John Belushi died young and were the same way" (Timpone 2006).

While most clowns are marked by their face paint and distinctive costumes, there are exceptions. For example clowns in the Archaos Circus—a short-lived (1986–1991) French troupe focusing on sideshow acts—wore no traditional clown makeup, but instead performed a blend of traditional circus and carnival sideshows acts rooted in the surrealism of Salvador Dali and René Magritte. In his book *A-Z of Horror*, Clive Barker quotes "Jason Covatch, a clown with the anarchic circus Archaos. 'The natural response to terror is initially to laugh, which is why if a child fears that he or she is threatened they will laugh, because they're not actually aware of the possible violence and damage and pain'" (Barker 1997, 88).

The clown is a curious character partly because he or she combines the superficially contradictory human feelings of horror and humor. Most things that truly scare or terrify us are not funny; getting cancer, dying in a car accident, or drowning in a riptide are never mined for laughs by comics or clowns. "For the purposes of sensationalism, at least, killer clowns are an incredibly efficient image. Lurid and overly emphatic though they may be, by placing the pleasures of laughter in close proximity to mortal threat, they embody a particularly tense and volatile contradiction" (Stott 2012, 4).

With the emotional distance of a fictional depiction—a play, novel, or film—the otherwise scary acts of a clown may be funny. Horror comedies such as *Dead Alive*, *The Evil Dead*, and countless others manage to easily blend horror and comedy. Noel Carroll, discussing the interplay between humor and horror in the *Journal of Aesthetics and Art Criticism*, notes, "Standardly we do not laugh at our horrific monsters. . . . Fear must be directed at something that is perceived to be or believed to be harmful. One cannot be afraid of something that one does not believe is harmful. I cannot be afraid of a kidney bean, or if I am afraid of a kidney bean, then that must be due to the fact that I have some rather strange beliefs about kidney beans, e.g., that they are mind parasites from an alternative universe" (Carroll 1999, 150).

Carroll attributes fear of clowns in part to their inherent impurity and defiance of easy categorization. They are obviously human (underneath the unnaturally colored skin, wigs, and garish clothes) yet look distinctly inhuman. They are supposed to be funny, but are often scary. Clowns are liminal creatures that straddle categories, and thus make us uncomfortable, even if on a subconscious level—the way that any unknown person in disguise who stands near us or interacts with us might. This makes sense from an evolutionary psychology perspective: millennia ago letting a masked stranger of unknown origin and motive near you or into your tribe was an invitation for trouble.

Carroll notes that "the basis of comic amusement is incongruity—the bringing together of disparate or contrasting ideas or concepts. Comic teams, for example, are often composed of a tall, thin character and a short, fat one [e.g., Abbott and Costello, Penn and Teller]. And European clown performances are frequently comprised of an immaculately clean, sartorially fastidious white clown—the epitome of orderliness and civilizations—and an unruly, disheveled, hairy and smudged clown—the lord of disorder and mischief. . . . Comedy . . . takes hold in contexts where incongruous, contrasting, or conflicting properties are brought together for our attention" (Carroll 1999, 153). The humor comes from the contrast, the venerable "fish out of water" theme successfully mined by writers for centuries.

The polka dot–jumpsuited clown straddles these lines, and with giant red shoes in two worlds he makes us uneasy. We like to know where things stand, we like to divide the world into neat, predictable categories of good and bad, safe and harmful. Blurring those lines creates fear: Stephen King, for example, has often mined this theme in his horror novels where something familiar and innocuous is suddenly turned into an instrument of pain and death: a dog in *Cujo*, a car in *Christine*, and so on. But with a clown we're never really sure what we're going to get.

Clowns as Freaks and Supernatural

Not only are clowns often seen as freaks, some of them are in fact freaks. The parallels between circus or sideshow freaks and clowns are stronger than may be apparent at first glance. Not only did they often work together, but dwarfs on occasion performed as clowns; indeed, "In circus clowning, as carried on in Britain in the late 1970s, the fool and the midget performed together" (Carmeli 1989, 141). A dwarf clown was featured in the 1917 classic *Polly of the Circus*, and a photograph taken in 1951 depicts "midget clowns Paul Horomp and a colleague entertain two young visitors to the Barnum & Bailey's back lot" (Jando 2008, 238). (The term *midget* for dwarf—or better yet, little person—is now considered derogatory but is retained here in quotations.)

In 1975 anthropologist Yoram Carmeli did a study involving JS, a two-foot-five circus clown who traveled with British circuses in the 1960s and 1970s under the name Wee Pea. As a dwarf, JS was sometimes cast in skits in a dehumanizing role (for example as a monkey): "JS did not like his monkey roles, especially that of the monkey in the cage during the parade." On the other hand, Carmeli notes, the dwarf "was reluctant when he had to perform most distinctly as a human, that is, while talking, as this disclosed his human nature most and therefore—in the circus context—his deformity" (Carmeli 1989, 142). Indeed, his direct, non-performance interactions with the public were especially difficult for him because he was stripped of his protective clown persona. While under greasepaint and outlandish costumes JS was whatever the role called for him to be: a drunk bully, an angry policeman, or a pie thief.

But outside the tent in public it was a different matter, for

> the more JS was made to expose his real deformity, the more he was reduced as a human being to just being his small size. Midgetness became a total performance for the dwarf, constituting both his show and his central existential condition. When JS in costume stood in the big-top doors during the show's interval selling balloons, people would watch him closely. Children would approach him to pay, asking their mothers if he was a "real man." Mothers would sometimes allow their children to draw nearer and touch the circus midget and JS could only murmur to a circus man standing nearby: "Get them little bastards away from me." (Carmeli 1989, 143)

Thus we see another context in which the clowns' chameleonic character can serve as an insulating layer against the outside world.

Dwarves, like early clowns such as the Harlequin, were at times believed to be supernatural figures (for a fascinating look at Victorian-era belief about dwarves, see the chapter "Little Goblin Men" in Carole G. Silver's book *Strange and Secret Peoples: Fairies and Victorian Consciousness*), and thus it's not surprising that the connection, however latent, remains to this day. In the context of the 1970s British circus clown Wee Pea, "the midget's victories are accomplished through the clown's misunderstandings and by the tricky use of the smallness of his body. The midget is unexpectedly hiding, waiting to surprise. The clowns, the big ones, do not notice little Pea who cleverly [uses] his smallness to outwit them. . . . The midget, through the play of the clown, is less human, exceptionally small but seemingly omnipotent" (Carmeli 1989, 139).

In addition to dwarf clowns, there were even a few fake-freak clowns, such as a three-headed, two-armed, three-legged clown conglomeration that appears in H. Thomas Steele's book *1000 Clowns More or Less*. A photograph, taken in the 1950s, shows a fake clown head sticking up between two real clowns joined at the hip in a specially crafted costume, and might have looked unnervingly realistic from a distance, as most of the audience is in a three-ring circus.

While most bad clowns are merely scary men (and some women) in makeup, some evil clowns are supernatural beings. The sadistic film character Killjoy, for example, is a demonic entity, as is Pennywise in Stephen King's *It*; the Fat Clown in the *Spawn* comics is also a demon from deepest Hell. The depiction of clowns as supernatural or inhuman freaks is not surprising. As Noel Carroll notes,

> The clown figure is a monster. . . . It is a fantastic being, one possessed of an alternate biology, a biology that can withstand blows to the head by hammers and bricks that would be deadly for any mere human, and the clown can sustain falls that would result in serious injury for the rest of us. Not only are clowns exaggeratedly misshapen and, at times, outright travesties of the human form—contortions played on our paradigms of the human shape—they also possess a physical resiliency conjoined with muscular and cognitive dysfunctionalities that mark them off as imaginary species. (Carroll 1999, 155)

Freaks and dwarves, unlike other clowns, cannot remove their makeup and costume to thus return to normalcy. Perhaps even more terrifying than a clown identity that you can adopt and remove at will is one that you can't remove at all. Michael Chabon explored this theme in his celebrated short story "The God of Dark Laughter." Set in a rural western Pennsylvania town, the story tells of the curious investigation by a district attorney of a dead clown found in nearby woods. The corpse, "dressed in a mad suit of purple and orange velour," had been shot and the murderer "skinned his head from chin to crown and clavicle to clavicle, taking ears, eyelids, lips, and scalp in a single grisly flap, like the cupped husk of a peeled orange." Upon making inquiries, the investigator notes, "I gathered, reading between the lines, that clowns were high-strung types, and not above going off on the occasional bender. This poor fellow had probably jumped ship here two weeks ago, holing up somewhere with a case of rye, only to run afoul of a very nasty person, possibly one who harbored no great love of clowns" (Chabon 2001). The district attorney follows clues implicating an ancient cult of clown worshippers whose apparent snowy pallor did not come from an eight-ounce disc of standard Mehron-brand Clown White theatrical makeup, but instead from a genetic pigmentation disease such as vitiligo. The man is, in the words of one writer, a biological clown, "*un clown biologique*" (Rotella 2004).

We have seen many psychological reasons for uneasiness with clowns, though in his book *The Pyrotechnic Insanitarium* cultural critic Mark Dery offers another theory: that that the seemingly widespread unease with clowns is due in part to their useful role as a "societal scapegoat." Dery seems to overstate his case that "the symbolic sacrifice of a pie-facing, pratfalling agent of chaos is a means of appeasing the turbulent forces that seem to be pulling our world off its axis"—surely there are far more salient and direct scapegoats than clowns for America's social problems (such as illegal immigrants or drug users)—though he offers an interesting example of the depiction: "[Artist] John Bergin takes the theme of clown-as-whipping boy to extremes. Wedding fantasies of clown abuse to a universal symbol of ritual scapegoating, his 1990 cover painting for the underground comic *Caliber Presents* [see plate 2] depicts the feet of a crucified clown, his goofy, oversized shoes transfixed by a nasty-looking nail" (Dery 1999, 66).

CHAPTER 4

Coulrophobia

Fear of Clowns

A nything bad is unpleasant or dangerous in some way, and bad clowns are no exception. Thus it makes sense that some people fear bad clowns. Hating, or being afraid of, clowns is remarkably common— or at least that's the perception.[1]

Various celebrities including Johnny Depp, Billy Bob Thornton, and P. Diddy (a.k.a Puff Daddy, a.k.a Sean Combs) are said to fear clowns. Famous fictional characters do too: on the *Seinfeld* episodes "The Opera" (airdate November 4, 1992) and "The Gymnast" (airdate November 3, 1994) the character Cosmo Kramer is revealed to fear clowns. Alexander "Xander" Harris, friend of Buffy the Vampire Slayer on the popular series of the same name, has feared clowns since his sixth birthday when a clown chased him, as revealed in the episode "Nightmares" (airdate May 12, 1997).

Wakko Warner, the sibling of Yakko and Dot Warner of the 1993–1998 animated television show *Animaniacs*, fears clowns (as does fictional Warner Bros. CEO Thaddeus Plotz). Wakko's fear of clowns is most evident in the episode "Clown and Out," (airdate July 23, 1993) in which a wacky clown (shrieking a Jerry Lewis–esque catchphrase "Hey Laydeeee!") chases Wakko and Plotz around the Warner Bros. lot. Mime Time, an occasional segment on *Animaniacs*, featured as a recurring gag an annoyingly happy mime who is repeatedly squashed (usually with heavy objects falling from above) for simply doing his job silently and without complaint.

FIGURE 4.1. A clown frightens Warner Bros. studio head Thaddeus Plotz in "Clown and Out," an episode of *Animaniacs*. 1995 Topps trading card set number 62, from the author's collection.

This pathological disdain for mimes has appeared in other contexts as well, including the film *Shakes the Clown*. Bart Simpson of *The Simpsons* is also afraid of clowns, though unlike Wakko, Bart's concern is not a phobia; instead he has legitimate reason to be fearful, since Krusty the Clown's former sidekick, Robert Underdunk Terwilliger—better known as Sideshow Bob—has tried to murder the boy on and off for decades. Bart Simpson's fear of clowns became an integral, rather than an incidental, part of the character: a famous episode featured a wide-eyed (even by *Simpsons* standards) and terrified Bart saying, "Can't sleep, clown'll eat me." This image and catchphrase about cannibalistic clowns later appeared on T-shirts, coffee mugs, and other pop culture merchandise, bought and beloved by those for whom clown fear is hip and humorous.

Sharing the Love, Spreading the Fear

Scary Clowns, a short humor book featuring a wide variety of clown photos, discusses fear of clowns in its introduction:

The term coulrophobia—fear of clowns—has come into common usage only in the past two decades. Now there are numerous support groups and hundreds of web sites dedicated to the fear. "I Hate Clowns" sites encourage people to share their fear and hatred online. There is a web site dedicated to real anti-clown news, which is full of stories concerning clowns who have abused children, stolen things, killed, robbed banks, or defrauded normal, God-fearing people. You can buy anti-clown T-shirts, pins, cards, and hats. There are coulrophobic blogs and therapy courses. And they don't all originate in America; there are British, German, Scandinavian, and Eastern European anti-clown sites. (*Scary Clowns* 2006)

The book argues that "part of the rise of coulrophobia can be blamed on the increasing use of clowns in slasher horror films. Since the early 1980s, a string of movies has been made in which the central, murderous character is a clown." While it is true that evil clowns have become more popular in recent decades, there's no clear evidence that fear of clowns is in fact on the rise; we have no reliable polls or surveys from yesteryear asking people whether or not they found clowns scary. Simply put, nobody thought to ask great-great-grandpa if he soiled his britches at the sight of clowns during the Taft administration. Horse-carriage accidents and tuberculosis were probably of far greater concern to our forefathers than painted circus men in colorful costumes.

It is certainly true that bad clowns have become more common in pop culture over the past few decades, but that doesn't necessarily reflect a corresponding increase in fear of those characters. As any scientist can tell you, correlation does not imply causation—that is, genuine fear of clowns may have led to more scary fictional clowns in pop culture, or more scary fictional clowns in pop culture may have led to more fear of clowns in real people, or both, or neither. Epidemiologists know that sometimes a rise in the reported incidence of a condition or disease does not necessarily reflect any actual increase, but instead can be attributed to other factors such as newly expanded diagnostic criterion, more accurate testing methods, or simply more public awareness of the issue. Thus the increase in evil clowns in popular fiction since the 1980s is not a reliable measure of the public's fear of clowns. It is perhaps telling that

Scary Clowns, one of only a handful of books on the subject, is a humor book; its discussion is, at best, tongue-in-cheek and hardly scholarly.

It's important to draw a distinction between coulrophobia (which, like all phobias, is an irrational fear) and fear of scary or threatening clowns (such as Pennywise in Stephen King's classic *It*.) The premise of many horror films is to make something familiar into something threatening. A man on the street corner using a chainsaw to cut a fallen tree is not a threat; that same man chasing you with the chainsaw is a real threat. Being afraid of a clown making balloon dogs at a circus is a clown phobia; being afraid of that same clown sadistically twisting a live dachshund into a grotesque, furry tube of spine and dripping gore is not. There is nothing at all odd, pathological, or unreasonable about fearing a clown chasing you with a gun or a meat cleaver.

Clinical Coulrophobia

If pop psychology doesn't provide a clear picture of clown fear, serious academic research doesn't help much. Coulrophobia, as such, is essentially nonexistent in the medical and psychological literature. A handful of professional journal articles mention it in passing, but by far the great bulk of references are to newspaper and magazine articles. Coulrophobia, as it is often used, is not actually a recognized clinical phobia; it is instead a sort of pop culture, pseudoclinical term.[2] While many consider it to be funny or hip to talk of fearing clowns, genuine phobia of clowns is rare. Though people who fear clowns may panic in the presence of clowns, the disorder is considered a phobia instead of a panic disorder unless the panic also happens unexpectedly (and, for example, the fear generalizes to anyone in face paint, makeup, or costume).

As for clinical coulrophobes, therapists who treat their client's fear of clowns typically do so using standard psychological techniques such as psychotherapy and habituation (gradually increasing exposure to the object of fear). In psychology, phobias are a subcategory of anxiety disorders, which affect between 2 percent and 4 percent of the general population. According to the American Psychiatric Association's *Diagnostic and Statistical Manual of Mental Disorders* (fifth edition), "The fear or anxiety is out of proportion to the actual danger that the object or situation poses, or more intense than is deemed necessary. Although individuals with specific phobia often recognize their reactions as disproportionate, they tend to overestimate the danger in feared situations. . . . In the United States, the 12-month community prevalence estimate for specific phobia is approximately 7 percent to 9 percent [though] rates are generally lower in Asian, African and Latin American countries (2 percent to 4 percent)" (American Psychiatric Association 2014, 201).

There are no reliable statistics on exactly how many people genuinely fear clowns, though it doesn't even crack the top ten most common phobias—such as arachnophobia (spiders), agoraphobia (open spaces), claustrophobia (small spaces), and acrophobia (heights)—thus it's certainly far below 1 percent of the general population and likely closer to half that. One Canadian journalist searched in vain for therapists who had coulrophobic patients: "Amy Janek, head of the anti-anxiety clinic at the University of British Columbia, has yet to see a clown case. The closest she's come was a woman who reported being unnerved by a costumed Easter Bunny in a store. In thirty years, psychologist Ralph Maddess . . . has seen only one patient with a clown problem. Her anxiety wasn't sparked so much by the sight of clowns, but the raucous sounds they sometimes make" (Gibson 2004).

As for how these fears come about,

Specific phobia sometimes develops following a traumatic event (e.g., being attacked by an animal or stuck in an elevator), observation of others going through a traumatic event (e.g., watching someone drown), an unexpected panic attack in the feared situation (e.g., an unexpected panic attack while on the subway), or informational transmission (e.g., extensive media coverage of a plane crash). However many individuals with specific phobia are unable to recall the specific reason for the onset of their phobias. Specific phobia usually develops in early childhood, with the majority of cases developing prior to age 10 years. The median age at onset is between 7 and 11 years, with the mean at about 10 years. (American Psychiatric Association 2014, 200)

This phobia criterion sheds light on coulrophobia. Many people do indeed trace their fear of clowns back to one specific, memorably unpleasant incident when a clown frightened them, for example at a circus or birthday party during their childhood. What is of perhaps even more interest are the other, indirect ways that such a phobia can be created: both by seeing other people menaced by clowns and what's rather stiltingly referred to as "informational transmission," and which could include seeing scary clowns in movies.

When we look at the approximate age range of children who would have seen scary films containing evil clowns, we can begin to trace back some of the fears. The film *Poltergeist* came out in 1982, for example, and children who were in their early teens at the time would now be in their early forties and remember the scary clown scene from the film; eight years later, Generation X kids who were in their early teens when killer clown Pennywise showed up in the 1990 TV miniseries *It* would have their own cultural childhood touchstone of clown fear. With the advent of VCRs and DVD players, of course, these and later evil-clown films can scare the hell out of new generations of children.

In these cases people don't see others being traumatized by evil clowns in real life, of course—they're actors in a scary movie. But many kids, especially between seven and eleven years old, may not fully differentiate real life from fictional stories the way adults do, and it's quite likely that many people's unpleasant feelings about clowns are often due not to personal experience but scary movies. Thus the clown fears are created, at least in part, by a cycle of pop culture influencing children, who then reinforce and highlight the frightening side of clowns.

The lack of information on fear of clowns specifically may be surprising given how often the subject is discussed (fear of clowns seems to come up almost as often as discussions of clowns themselves), but it's quite understandable from a clinical psychology perspective. For many people who suffer from phobias, the best treatment may be no treatment at all, but instead simply avoiding the subject they fear. If you have a fear of sharks, for example, you need not spend months or years in time-consuming and expensive professional therapy to overcome your fear since you can control your proximity to sharks. Similarly, most people who genuinely fear clowns don't bother to seek professional mental help because clowns are so easily avoided. (It's like the old joke where a person visits a doctor and says, "Can you please help me? I get an awful pain in

FIGURE 4.2. Evil-clown temporary tattoos, manufactured by DSG in 2006 and sold in coin vending machines. From the author's collection.

my neck when I cross my eyes and tilt my head way back and to the left like this." The doctor replies, "Sure, I can help. Don't do that.")

Fear of clowns exists, of course, but it's not a medically recognized serious issue causing significant disruption in most people's lives. Clowns—unlike spiders, small spaces, and flatulent coworkers—are easily avoided; they are typically only found in certain habitats such as circuses and parties. When they violate those proscribed social and geographical boundaries, as happened with the Northampton Clown and his ilk (see chapter 9), that's when people get upset. Coulrophobia is simply not a common enough (or serious enough) issue for clinical and research psychologists to spend a lot of time on—especially as compared to more common conditions that threaten quality of life, such as depression, anorexia, psychoses, schizophrenia, and so on.

The fact that bad and scary clowns are so popular suggests that most people are not in fact frightened of them—after all, if you're genuinely terrified of clowns you don't celebrate them, play with toys and figurines of them (such as the Joker; see plate 4), or get temporary tattoos of them.

Hospital Clowns

Straddling the line between good and bad clowns are hospital clowns. Hospitals are scary places; if the diseases and medicines don't kill you while you're there, the bill for twenty-dollar aspirin pills will likely finish you off. Unless you work in a hospital, the only reason you go there is if you are sick, injured, or dying—or know someone who is. In an effort to lighten the environment, many hospitals around the world have introduced clowns into the mix. The connections between clowning, psychological healing, and mythology have been studied (see, for example, Carp 1998), and the idea that therapeutic clowning can play a role in helping patients (often, though not exclusively, children) is a popular one.

An Australian doctor named Peter Spitzer, who also went by the name Dr. Fruit-Loop, wrote about hospital clowning in the medical journal *Lancet*: "Clowning in hospitals is not a new development. Several centuries ago in Turkey the Dervishes, who were responsible for the well being of patients, first fed the body then used their performance skills to feed the soul. The September 1908 issue of *Le Petit Journal* had on its cover a drawing of two clowns at work in a children's hospital ward in London. More recently, Patch Adams, as a young doctor in the 1970s, began clowning for hospital patients in Virginia, USA" (Spitzer 2008, 534). Spitzer, cofounder of a charity called the Humour Foundation, which arranges clown visits to clinical settings as part of their Clown Doctor Program, noted that hospital clowns are always professional performers—not medical doctors clowning around—and work no more than three days out of the week because of the taxing nature of the job. Spitzer described a typical visit: "Most often, gentle parody of the hospital routine works to reduce stress and anxiety for the patient. Laughter prescriptions are given, funny-bones are checked, red-nose transplants are done without anesthesia, and cat scans are enjoyed. There is no fixed routine, and improvisation ranks highly."

This is all well and good, but for some patients a clown is perhaps the least welcome visitor after the Grim Reaper. A 2008 article about hospital clowns noted that

> as the therapeutic clown works to support the child through play, humor, and empowering friendship, it is important that he or she keep

in mind the fact that some children, young people and adults are afraid of clowns, whether because of the unfamiliarity of the makeup and costuming, because of unfortunate incidents with unskilled and insensitive clowns or because of the fairly recent appearance of "evil clowns" in the media. . . . In order to address some of these issues, therapeutic clowns tend to present with minimal makeup and costuming. A red nose and a hat, and a visually pleasing costume are enough to communicate the clown's identity. . . . A well-trained therapeutic clown will watch for cues and react instantly if any sense of unease is present. (Koller and Grysnki 2008, 20–21)

How common is children's fear of clowns? Research suggests that, contrary to the popular idea of rampant adolescent coulrophobia, most kids enjoy clowns. A 2013 research article on patient and staff attitudes toward hospital clowns (Barkmann, Siem, Wessolowski, and Schulte-Markwort 2013) cited an Austrian study concluding that "the results of the evaluation were very positive overall. The clear majority of the children enjoyed the clown performances, wanted more frequent clown visits and preferred these to other entertainment activities on the ward. Only a small number of respondents reported feeling unwell or ill at ease or disturbed" by the clowns, and a British study determined that hospital clowns "showed a very positive reception by all groups. The vast majority (82%) of the children enjoyed the clown performances. Only 3 (6%) stated that they didn't like the clowns."

So if studies show that most children are fine with clowns—at least in a hospital setting where powerful sedatives are only a panicky nurse call away—what accounts for the common perception to the contrary? Part of it may be due to misleading or misunderstood headlines such as one in the *Telegraph* (UK) on December 26, 2007, titled "Children Are 'Scared of Hospital Clowns.'" The headline seems clear and unambiguous—except that the article is not referring to children's fear or dislike of actual clowns but instead clown *images* in hospital decor (such as on wallpaper and in art prints): "Hospitals are being urged not to decorate children's wards with paintings of clowns in case they upset young patients. State-funded research has found that in a survey of more than 250 children aged four to 16, all disliked the use of clowns in hospital decor, with even the teenagers seeing them as 'scary'" (Womack 2007). News stories about this study were "reported in the press as an indication that children do not like clowns, but then retracted when it was reported that this was about the use of clowns in the hospital decor rather than real clowns in live interactions" (Henderson and Rosario 2008, 984).

This "retraction" has unfortunately been largely ignored: a 2013 article on scary clowns for *Smithsonian* magazine seems to intentionally blur the lines between children being scared of clowns and children being scared of clown images: "Even the people who are supposed to like clowns—children—supposedly don't. In 2008, a widely reported University of Sheffield, England, survey of 250 children between the ages of four and 16 found that most of the children disliked and even feared images of clowns" (McRobbie 2013b); and a June 2014 article in the magazine *Mental Floss* repeated the misinformation: "In 2008, a study of 250 children concluded, 'Clowns are universally disliked.'" The myth that children hate clowns is apparently too good a story to let die, and in some cases popular news stories exaggerate the public's fear of clowns, likely legitimizing fears in the process.

CHAPTER 5

Bad Clowns of the Ink

Comic books, magazines, and graphic novels are natural places to find clowns, bad or otherwise. Clowns have populated comics since the early days (from Dell's *Bozo* and Marvel's *Slapstick* to Bill Griffith's *Zippy the Pinhead*), but the bad ones are relative newcomers to the entertainment media scene. There is of course significant crossover between books, comics, television, and films, with characters fluidly changing media all the time. The Joker, for example, was originally a comic book villain but gained global prominence on television and film screens. This chapter focuses on bad clowns whose evil antics have largely been confined to the printed page. Many have appeared in horror and crime fiction dating back decades (see, for example, plate 5).

Obnoxio the Clown

A year after a scary clown appeared in the horror film *Poltergeist*, Marvel Comics introduced Obnoxio the Clown in a special one-shot comic book, headlining along with one of its most popular titles, the X-Men. Obnoxio was tame by today's standards; he didn't freebase cocaine or try to kill children with his souped-up ice-cream truck (this was Marvel Comics, after all). But he was an obnoxious clown and clearly unfit for even the most temperamental problem child's birthday party.

Obnoxio was created by Larry Hama around 1979 and was drawn by Alan Kupperberg. Obnoxio is chronically behind on his bills and with great reluctance moonlights as a clown to help pay his rent. Social conventions are about as foreign to Obnoxio as personal hygiene, and he is pathologically contemptuous, bitter, short-tempered, and generally rude to everyone he meets.

Obnoxio wears a torn green costume with red (or sometimes black) polka dots, often stained with what could be anything from spoiled milk to horse semen. Obnoxio is unshaven, unkempt, and his head features a variety of dermal discharges characteristic of medieval European peasants in the final throes of bubonic plague. He is often sweaty and routinely chews a foul-smelling cigar. He wears ripped white gloves and sometimes employs a squirting rose that may or may not contain urine. He has the classic dual cones of hair on either side of his head like Krusty the Clown. His undersized, floppy green hat is adorned not only with a knife and a star (a classic cartoon trope signifying pain) but also prominent pirate-style skull and crossbones, which seems ironic only if you know nothing else about him. A clown in the Robert Williams painting *Two-Fisted Buffoons* (see chapter 7 and plate 16) is also adorned with a similar skull and crossbones pattern.

Obnoxio and *Crazy*

Obnoxio appeared as a mascot for *Crazy* magazine (1973 to 1983), a *MAD* magazine clone. In those pages Obnoxio was not merely obnoxious but in fact violent and often homicidal. In his *Crazy* encounters with objects of his satire, he is often seen with implements of destruction, including guns (shooting at J. R. Ewing in a 1981 cover parodying the famous "Who shot J. R.?" cliffhanger), axes (threatening *The Shining*'s Torrance family—see plate 6), flamethrowers (burning a caveman of *Quest for Fire*), chainsaws, and so on. On the cover of his 1983 one-shot comic *Obnoxio the Clown*, he holds the (apparently) lifeless body of beloved X-Man Kitty Pryde, saying, "Hiya kids! What's yellow and black and don't breathe no more?" This is followed by an asterisk that gives the answer to the riddle at the bottom of the page: a dead school bus.

Those who corresponded with Obnoxio via his various *Crazy* contests were fair game for abuse. Obnoxio walked a fine line between (apparently) feigned and sincere contempt for his "fans" and the magazine's readers. He had a regular feature in the magazine titled Obnoxio's Abuse Column, which contained a disclaimer: "Warning: Sending letters to this column indicates the sender's willingness to be abused. Publicly. Where all the sender's friends and relatives can see. Right here." That was no idle threat: a typical response to a contributor asks, "Why's yer letter in pencil, John? Run outta crayons? Y'know, you write like a sissy. I mean yer words are all weak-lookin'. You play with dolls, John? You like the ones that cry or the ones that wet all over ya? Well? Why does yer letter smell like perfume?"

A handful of Obnoxio the Clown Fun Pages appeared in *Crazy* and elsewhere, usually involving a jaded Obnoxio inviting kids to do lame "fun activities," like "Find the Identical Twin Derelict!" ("Use your powers of observation to pick out the hobos that are alike!") and count the number of bees (e.g., tiny dots) in a drawing of killer bees swarming around a terrified little girl named Suzy.

Crazy magazine occasionally held contests encouraging readers to submit jokes and cartoons. Like most magazines they printed the names of the winners; unlike most magazines *Crazy*'s Obnoxio took delight in those who were too stupid to send their entries on time: "Getting on to other dumbasses, these are the LOSERS of my Straw Poll Contest, that is they all sent in their submissions way past deadline. C'mon, gang, I got enuff paperwork without this," and he then cruelly ridiculed several readers by publishing their names and hometowns.[1]

It seems the staff at *Crazy* used Obnoxio to vent their spleens and air their personal and professional grievances. For example the December 1980 issue of Obnoxio's abuse column began,

Okay, gang, I'm really mad this month. Y'know why? Well, last month one of th' editors here at *Crazy* tried to get a few measely publicity photos of a T.V. show from a major television network. Y' know what? This network gave our editor th' runaround for almost two weeks . . . and then decided not to give him the photos! I tell ya, gang, I just can't figure it. I mean, here we go offerin' free publicity to a third-rate show on a third-rate network, and they turn us down? . . . Maybe their moms all dropped 'em when they were babies and gave 'em brain damage or somethin'. I know that not everybody who works for that network has the brain of a fish and the disposition of a brick. It just seems that way. Sorry I can't tell ya which network I'm steamed at, but I'm a nice guy. Oh, and by the way, I'd like to thank ABC and CBS fer all them nice publicity photos they've always supplied us.

If you understand the magazine it's clear what the editors are—that is, Obnoxio is—talking about. Film and television satires are one of the staples of magazines like *Mad, Crazy,* and *Cracked.* In order to write and illustrate a piece on it, a writer needs to see a sample show (often a sneak preview if it's a film), and an artist (usually a caricaturist such as Mort Drucker, Tom Richmond, or John Severin) needs to have photographs to draw the characters from. Decades later the Internet would provide artists with easy access to hundreds of photos of actors and celebrities, but in the 1980s magazines were at the mercy of film and television studio publicity departments to give them material to use, under the premise that a spoof (especially a front-cover spoof) was essentially free advertising for their TV show or film.

One of the TV networks—obviously NBC, since at the time there were only three networks and Obnoxio thanked the other two—had been contacted by a *Crazy* editor (likely editor Larry Hama or associate editor Jim Owsley) asking for publicity photos to provide an artist for a satire and gotten an unceremonious and frustrating runaround. In the following issue a pissed-off Obnoxio took aim at the brain-damaged executives, those of piscine intellect and dubious hygiene at an unnamed third-rate network with third-rate shows. It would seem unprofessional if Hama or Owsley (of *Crazy* magazine, published by image-conscious Marvel Comics) publicly lambasted a TV network for their unresponsiveness, but under the social license afforded clowns as truth tellers the editorial team employed Obnoxio to spew some very real-world venom and abuse.

Obnoxio dropped from the public eye for years, though he returned in the 2013 animated video *Marvel Super Heroes: What the—?! Obnoxio the Clown Returns,* in which Doctor Strange fails to entertain the X-Men at a party for Cyclops and so summons Obnoxio. Soon Obnoxio turns

FIGURE 5.1. Obnoxio the clown appears in a 2013 stop motion–animated video featuring the X-Men. Screen capture from YouTube video *Marvel Super Heroes: What the—?! Obnoxio the Clown Returns*.

on the sniveling Sorcerer Supreme, kicking his butt to the ground and then producing a baseball bat and mercilessly beating the cowering Strange as blood spatters with each sickening thwack and the X-Men cheer him on. It seems that the only thing the team of mutants like less than an obnoxious, vicious clown is a lame magician.

Though clowns play the fool, they're usually smarter (and even more bitter) than they look. Obnoxio comics are littered with literary references, including allusions to Ray Bradbury, George Burns, and "Uncle Floyd" Vivino—who was also the subject of a 2002 David Bowie song called "Slip Away," from his album *Heathen*. In 2001, Uncle Floyd appeared in a cameo as an announcer in a bad clown film by Insane Clown Posse titled *Big Money Hustlas*.

As seen in his comic book, Obnoxio lives in a run-down New York City apartment with ratty furniture, empty wine bottles and papers strewn on the floor, along with what appears to be at least one rat and an armadillo. In a 2007 interview Alan Kupperberg listed Obnoxio as one of the highlights of his comics career: "Well, there's the wonderful *Obnoxio the Clown Meets the X-Men* number one. I don't know if that's a high point. Script, pencils, inks, lettering and color. Or to quote Peter

David, 'Untouched by human hands.' Peter, take a long look in a mirror and consider the possible power of words to hurt. All the work I did for Marvel was a great deal of fun. The more control I had over it, the more fun I had" (Kupperberg and Cooke 2007).

Frenchy the Clown

No discussion of bad—or at least severely maladjusted—clowns would be complete without Frenchy. Frenchy the Clown was created and written by Nick Bakay, a *National Lampoon* contributing editor, actor, and comedy writer who went on to work on *In Living Color*, *Sabrina the Teenage Witch*, *The King of Queens*, and other series.

Written in the late 1980s and early 1990s, the Evil Clown stories in *National Lampoon* were illustrated by Alan Kupperberg and featured a grizzled clown named Frenchy. Frenchy wears white and red face paint, a tiny hat cocked to one side above a round fringe of red hair. Kupperberg was no stranger to the bitter side of clowns, having previously collaborated with Larry Hama to create Obnoxio the Clown. Where Obnoxio had to respect some decorum (appearing in ostensibly family-friendly funny pages), Frenchy gleefully pushed the boundaries of taste and acceptance.

For example, the cover of *Evil Clown Comics* number 7 (September 1991; see plate 7) finds our antihero around a summer campfire sharing a classic scary story. This is not about ghosts, snipes, or hook-handed serial killers, however: "Then this toothless hillbilly says, 'Take off your pants an' squeal like a pig!'" A huge bear is sneaking up behind Frenchy and as a child camper tries to alert him, he growls, "Chill out. . . . We haven't even gotten to the scary part yet." This is of course a reference to the notorious male rape scene from the classic 1972 Academy Award–winning John Boorman film *Deliverance*—a story very likely not on any officially approved list of campfire tales.

The tale, "In-A-Gadda-Da-Frenchy! (The Call of the Wild)," begins with Frenchy standing on a street corner in front of New York's Port Authority Bus Terminal. He is a street washer, the kind who squeegees windows on cars stopped in traffic and demands a tip for the effort whether the services are requested or not—and under the implied threat that a phlegmy, biohazardous bolus may appear on the newly cleaned window if a tip is not promptly forthcoming. A limousine arrives, and as another homeless man heads to take the job, Frenchy pulls out a knife and warns, "Back off, you fucking statistic." Someone in the limo tosses a few dollars at Frenchy, and the next panel shows a presumably postcoital Frenchy in a seedy flophouse with a prostitute. She asks sweetly, "So, Mister Clown-Man, how come your hallway always smell like pee?"

In the foreground Frenchy—busy lighting a crack pipe—takes little notice of the twisted stew of dried bodily fluids around them and replies, "Ease up, Aphrodite, I just want one more ticket to the hall of mirrors here."[2] Frenchy takes a job as a summer camp counselor for inner-city kids, and it pretty much degenerates from there, with references to pornography and masturbation, a child's limb being eaten by a wolf, a rival camper taking an arrow to his eye, Frenchy confessing to the camping kids in a game of Truth or Dare that he "once killed a man for sport," and so on.

Evil Clown Comics, a balls-to-the-wall three-ring circus of id-spewing depravity, soon became one of *National Lampoon*'s most popular features. Kupperberg makes no apologies for Frenchy's raunch: "In *comic books* it's offensive, but in real life, it's just real life. Spider-Man is not real life. The Evil Clown is real life. It is for adults. I've lived in New York City proper since the 1970s through to this day, and I'm telling you, the clown stories are real life. It's not *everyone's* life, but real people live as Frenchy does. Who lives like Peter Parker?" Kupperberg asks. Once again we see the Everyman element to clowns—we identify not with the spider-bitten superhero teenager but with the bitter and disgruntled outsider vicariously acting out our collective discontent.

I asked writer Nick Bakay how Frenchy and *Evil Clown Comics* came about. "It actually started when I was a contributing editor at the *National Lampoon*," he told me. "I was one of the more prolific contributors to the faux 'letter to the editor' page, and one of the more popular 'letters' I came up with read:

Sirs,
You know what the best part of the job is?
Getting kids with stitches in their stomachs to laugh too hard.
Evil Clown
Children's Hospital

That sick-joke mix of passive-aggressive sadism struck a nerve and "it wasn't long before we decided that might make a pretty disturbing comic."

Bakay (2006) admitted that he's afraid of clowns

> to my core. . . . I always found clowns *uber*-creepy. They used to come on *The Ed Sullivan Show* when I was really little, and even then I kept thinking, "Okay, not funny, kind of sadistic—what the hell am I missing?" When I was in college I sent away for a clown ventriloquist doll that was advertised in *TV Guide*. When it came, it was a small, cheap, plastic piece of shit—but that didn't stop me from breaking it out during drunken rampages and adding a raspy, angry voice. I named him "Frenchy"; he was an alcoholic house painter whose soul was trapped in a dummy, and, therefore, hyperabusive—people were amused for the first half hour, then I was on my own. I guess it always stayed in my subconscious, just waiting for a bigger canvas.

The keys to Frenchy's character were "rage, pathological narcissism, and a nice turn of phrase," Bakay said, and when asked if he was concerned about drawing too deep from the clownish fount of seltzered depravity he replied, "I was young enough not to really consider the impact of such things going out into the world, yet remained slightly awed that everything made it through editing [i.e., censoring] unscathed . . . until the final comic, which followed an editorial change at the magazine, when some pretty douchey, unproven Harvard kids started sharing their wisdom. That was that."

The creator of one of the most hilariously foul clowns to taint a magazine page was less than impressed by most of the bad clowns that followed: "Shakes and Homey both came after Frenchy, and both lacked any wallop for me. The bottom line is, no fictitious evil clown can hold a candle to the innate creepiness of a sincere clown—they are the worst."

Like the moribund rock group Spinal Tap, Frenchy seems to be currently residing in the "Where are they now?" file. Despite a handful of aborted attempts to collect and republish *Evil Clown Comics*, it seems that the project is dead in Frenchy's bong water. According to Kupperberg, "In 1994 *Heavy Metal* was going to publish a collection of the Evil Clown stories. I didn't feel that the artwork on the first two stories was up to par with the rest of the stories. So I re-lettered and re-drew them. The project did not go forward because Nick didn't seem to be interested in signing the contracts or something like that. I don't know what it was" (Best 2007). Perhaps one day Frenchy will resume his depraved, childhood-tainting ways, but until then his exploits can be found in *Evil Clown Comics*.

Beautiful Stories for Ugly Children

Though lesser known than either Obnoxio or Frenchy, bad clowns also make an appearance in the premiere issue of the 1989–1992 comic book series *Beautiful Stories for Ugly Children* (see plate 8), published by Piranha Press (an imprint of DC Comics). Written by Dave Louapre and illustrated by Dan Sweetman, the first issue was titled *A Cotton Candy Autopsy* and involves hairless dogs, freaky sex (not merely kinky sex, but sex with freaks, which I suppose covers both bases), an angry clown ruining a child's birthday party, and a clown whose bloating body is torn between the ravages of rigor mortis and the desiccating desert heat. It's sort of like something you might find in the original Grimm's fairy tales if they included dead clowns.

The story begins: "The circus was burning. It was me, Bingo, Foo Foo, and Joey Punchinello from the street. Foo Foo stole the keys to the Dart while Bingo grabbed Addy the Freaklady and some of our best pups. I got the booze out the ringmaster's trailer when he was watching the big top burn. Joey Punchinello just lay low. Everyone knew he was always wiser to things than he was saying, like when that midget got drowned in the horse trough last winter."

Thus begins a twisted road trip that's soon interrupted when one of the clowns, Foo Foo, runs into a motorcycle gang and gets beaten nearly to death ("I'm telling you, if the clown has a natural enemy, it's bikers"). In a scene reminiscent of Robert Williams's classic painting *Two-Fisted Buffoons* (see chapter 7) Addy the two-headed lady watches as clowns and bikers duke it out not far from a burning circus tent: "She used to be wild for those bare-knuckle clown fights behind the tents after hours, but this was different to her, I guess."

The Foo is not long for this world—due to biker-induced internal hemorrhaging and a damaged liver that was far from pristine to begin with—and then a second classic clown rivalry raises its head: "That's when we saw that stinking mime, mugging like he's in some box that ain't there and leaning against some phony wind. It hit us all at the same time that he should die . . . and when I gun it out of that drive-thru, the crowd around this idiot scatters like a dream and BAM!—Bingo smacks a bottle of scotch in his face and sends him flying, and we tear off down the highway listening for sirens that never come."

It's not clear whether the sirens never come because the clowns got away or because the police tacitly approve of mime murder—one less lowlife whose right to remain silent would be wasted with an unnecessary Miranda warning. In any event the clowns' joyride takes them on a road to brutality, madness, love, and death.

Spawn's Violator/Clown

The Image Comics series *Spawn*, created by Todd MacFarlane, features a demon named Violator who appears on Earth in the form of a clown called Clown. Introduced in the second issue of the series (May 1992), Clown is squat, obese, and vile, with a blue M-shaped mark on his face (see plate 9). The character is mostly clown in name only and Spawn's best-known archenemy, with various supernatural powers, including great strength, telepathy, breathing fire, and the ability to change form. Violator/Clown was portrayed by John Leguizamo in the widely panned 1997 film adaptation of the comic.

There are a handful of other bad clowns in games and toys worthy of note. Perhaps the most iconic video-game clown is Sweet Tooth, of the *Twisted Metal* video-game series for PlayStation. The play action takes place in vehicular combat during a demolition derby, with each player choosing their own vehicle and weapons. The serial-killing Sweet Tooth, whose real name is name Marcus "Needles" Kane, drives an ice-cream truck—of course—and has appeared on the cover of every *Twisted Metal* game to date.

More maladjusted clowns can be found in the Hispanic/Latino culture, in the form of Homie Clowns, a subset of the popular Homies line of toy figures and characters introduced by California-based artist David

FIGURE 5.2. (*top*) Instruction manual for *Twisted Metal* video-game series featuring the evil clown Sweet Tooth. From the author's collection.

FIGURE 5.3. (*bottom*) Three in a series of Homie Clowns by California-based artist David Gonzales. From the author's collection.

Gonzales (see figure 5.3). On his website Gonzales explains that they are "a band of dysfunctional outcast clowns. Banned from performing at any respectable circuses, they have formed their own traveling show called the Homie clown Circus. Performing underground illegal freak shows nightly in abandoned warehouses to a background of heavy metal and hip-hop music, the Homie clowns are always one step ahead of law enforcement. Keep an eye out—the Homie clowns may be hitting your hood next!" Each of the Homie Clowns has distinctive features and backgrounds, with names including Cereal, Loco, 2face, Hobo, Pyro, Jester, Vato, Pogo, and Manic, and can be found in bubble-gum vending machines across North America.

CHAPTER 6

Bad Clowns of the Screen

Though print media have long been home to bad clowns, film and television are perhaps more influential because of their mass-media reach. With fewer and fewer people reading books these days (thank you for reading—better yet buying—this one), more people are being scared by clowns in visual media. Movie clowns tend to be far more violent and abusive than television clowns for various reasons, including that the media depicting them are very different. Films can get away with much more explicit content than broadcast television.

It is not possible, of course, to include every film that stars or features an evil clown. Any sort of "comprehensive" list would soon be out of date, and little more than an unhelpful laundry list of references ranging from *It* to the infamously troll-free *Troll 2*. The focus here is on especially socially and culturally significant evil clowns. There is much overlap between bad clowns in books and bad clowns in films since many books featuring the clowns have been turned into movies, and many novelizations have been made from films.

One of the earliest motion pictures involving a bad clown was *He Who Gets Slapped*, the 1924 silent film in which Lon Chaney Sr. plays Paul Beaumont, a scientist on the verge of making an important breakthrough. A wealthy baron becomes his patron, who soon not only takes credit for Beaumont's ideas but, adding indignity to injury, slaps him in front of academic colleagues when confronted. Beaumont then seeks solace in the arms of his wife saying, "He slapped me, Marie. I would have killed him, but they laughed—laughed as if I were a clown." Yet she too betrays him with a slap, admitting an affair with the baron. Clown slapping and public humiliation become a running theme.

Five years later we revisit Beaumont, who is now performing as a circus clown named "HE who gets slapped" and masochistically enduring slaps and humiliations by other clowns. He muses rhetorically about the nature of cruelty and sadism: "What is it in human nature that makes people quick to laugh when someone else gets slapped—whether the slap be spiritual, mental, or physical?" Beaumont soon falls in love with a fellow performer, but when he once again is betrayed (and once again slapped with enthusiastic abandon) he finally takes revenge on those who abused him.

If there's an expert on scary clowns in films and on television, it's Tony Timpone, the longtime editor of *Fangoria* magazine. I asked him about his experience with scary and killer clowns: "Personally as a child I was never scared by clowns and I wasn't aware of any particular killer clown subgenre," he said. "I think the first time I saw a malevolent or scary-looking clown was probably Lon Chaney Sr., seeing him in his makeup in the silent film *Laugh, Clown, Laugh* [1928]. Then there was *Poltergeist*—I thought the clown puppet in *Poltergeist* [see plate 10] was very scary, even though it wasn't a human clown, when it comes to life and hides under the bed."

When a remake of *Poltergeist* was released in 2015, the appeal of the evil clown was not lost on the film's marketing department, and the studio capitalized on the now-iconic evil-clown doll. Whereas it only made a brief appearance in the original film—and was virtually absent in the movie trailer (the lanky doll is briefly glimpsed twice as nothing more than set dressing)—the clown played a prominent role in promoting the remake; not only was the creepy doll highlighted in the trailer and posters for the 2015 film, but one of the poster versions even depicted the evil-clown doll and nothing else—notable since the film is about ghosts, not clowns.

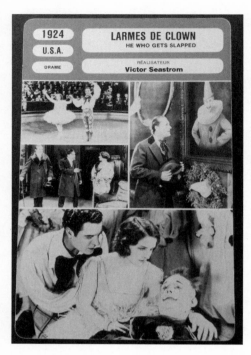

FIGURE 6.1. (*top*) French film card for *Larmes De Clown* (*He Who Gets Slapped*), 1924. From the *Les Fiches de Monsieur Cinema* series. From the author's collection.

FIGURE 6.2. (*bottom*) An evil-clown doll featured on a poster for the 2015 version of *Poltergeist*.

"It made *Bravo's 100 Scariest Movie Moments* television series, and I think it deserved it," Timpone added. "And the movie that took an over-the-top approach was *Killer Klowns from Outer Space*, which was a very entertaining B-movie approach, a real tribute to the 1950s style science fiction movies" (Timpone 2006). Indeed, for many people the evil-clown genre really began with *Killer Klowns from Outer Space*.

Killer Klowns from Outer Space (1988)

Killer clowns! From outer space! Holy shit!

—Mooney, *Killer Klowns from Outer Space*

"Bad clowns? Is there any other kind?" asks Edward Chiodo with a laugh. Chiodo—along with his brothers Stephen and Charles—were behind the classic bad-clown movie *Killer Klowns from Outer Space* (Chiodo 2007). The 1988 film, made for about $2 million, was grade-B camp but grade-A entertainment and introduced evil clowns to American pop culture.

The action takes place in the sleepy rural town of Crescent Cove. Two teens see a UFO land, and upon investigating find not a crashed saucer but a circus tent. Armed with cotton-candy weapons, popcorn bazookas, and a bizarre balloon-animal dog, the aliens (who look like grotesque clowns, designed by Charles; see plate 11), terrorize the town.

Despite lackluster promotion and a very limited theatrical release, *Killer Klowns from Outer Space* was a modest success at the time, buoyed in part by the title song, which was written and performed by the Dickies and released the same year. The film gained new life and a new set of fans on cable TV and with the spread of videotapes. It became a cult classic, and twenty-five years after their genre-defining film (and scads of imitators), the Brothers Chiodo are pleased that their Killer Klowns are still relevant. "We didn't set out to make a hit, or necessarily make it popular," Edward told me. "We make movies that we like. We had fun making them, and used images that spoke to us and that we were really fond of." Stephen added, "I'm still amazed at how many people like it, and who say it had an impact on them. The fact that it found its audience validates the things we like." *Killer Klowns* has been very influential, not only for B-movie buffs but also for many B-movie filmmakers and others; as

Stephen noted, "When we look at Halloween costumes now and many scary clowns in movies, all the images of scary clowns seem to be derivatives of Charles's designs. . . . They're all based on that image of a sick, twisted maniacal clown" (Chiodo 2007).

The concept for the killer clowns came about as the result of a thought experiment by Edward Chiodo: "I was thinking about what was the most frightening image I could imagine. To me, it was driving down a lonely mountain road all by yourself, and having a car come by, passing you. When you look over, you see a clown with a maniacal smile and he laughs. To me, that was the most horrible image I could think of, what seemed to be an archetypal, primal fear" (Chiodo 2007). Charles then kicked up the creepiness by adding an alien element, asking what if the clown didn't pull up beside you but was instead floating in the air as if from outer space.

Stephen noted that some audiences have misunderstood the film's villains: "Some people and critics thought that aliens dressed up as clowns, and that's not the case. It's an alien race that just happens to look like what we call clowns. It's like [Superman's] Bizarro world; their world is just filled with carnival and circus motifs; that's just their culture. We never really say where they're from or what they are, but there was this hypothesis that circulated saying that maybe they were ancient astronauts that came to Earth centuries ago, and that's where our image of clowns comes from" (Chiodo 2007).

As for any fear of clowns, Edward says, "I was never afraid of clowns. I just never liked them, never thought they were funny, I didn't like their antics. To me, it was an unnerving thing. One of my first experiences with a clown was at Ringling Brothers at Madison Square Garden, and this clown came up to me and was doing all this big slapstick stuff right in my face, and I didn't like it. . . . I was kind of put off and frightened by it, but everyone around me was laughing. I thought, 'Why is everyone laughing? This is frightening!'" (Chiodo 2007). Turning childhood trauma (or at least annoyance) into creative gold, the Chiodos are still active in filmmaking; a sequel to *Killer Klowns from Outer Space* is slated to hit theaters in 2016.

Shakes the Clown (1991)

Though comic Bobcat Goldthwait may be best remembered for his wild-voiced appearances in the *Police Academy* movies of the 1980s, he has continued to write and direct films. Among them is perhaps the most famous bad-clown film in history: *Shakes the Clown*.

Goldthwait appears as the titular Shakes, a depressed and alcoholic party clown who is framed for a murder by a rival clown. Roger Ebert describes the setup: "Set in the mythical town of Palukaville, it penetrates the clown underground—a hard-drinking twilight world where clowns never take off their makeup, and sit around bars all day, bitching and moaning about their problems. Shakes, who has not been sober in recent memory, is one of the most troubled clowns, passing out in strange bathrooms and trying to fake his way through kiddie birthday parties while fighting killer hangovers" (Ebert 1992). Shakes must try to clear his name while getting his life together, reuniting with his lost love, and working in time to harass mimes.

Shakes the Clown, aptly described as "the *Citizen Kane* of alcoholic clown movies" by Betsy Sherman of the *Boston Globe*, is not a masterpiece by any standard, though Goldthwait packs a constellation of bad-clown tropes into his film. Those clichés are exploited with Goldthwaitish glee but most of his targets are low-hanging fruit such as alcoholism, depression, drug use, and promiscuity. Laughing at a hungover clown struggle his hazy way through a kid's birthday party is like cooing at the cuteness of an Anne Geddes photograph of a giggling, flower-potted baby. If you can't make a wasted clown funny or a baby look cute, then you're not even trying.

The film is notable for not simply using Shakes as a one-note bad-clown gag but exploring the character in his own world. *Shakes the Clown*'s discussion of the social tensions between clowns and mimes is a gold mine for the amateur armchair anthropologist. Clowns have typically fought with mimes for a position on the lowest rungs of the circusian social strata and busker circuits. The clown-mime rivalry appears in *Shakes the Clown* as a sort of gang warfare, and the film features a cameo by Robin Williams as a mime instructor. The film includes a credit for the character Beaten Mime in Park, which gives you a clue about its tone.

In her book *Bring On the Clowns*, Beryl Hugill noted that Woody Allen, no fan of mimes, "has said that he was never quite sure whether the wispy white-faced figure darting about the stage was spreading a picnic blanket or milking a goat" (Hugill 1980, 191).

Goldthwait, to his credit, has often been drawn to dark-comedy themes that most writers and directors would fear to touch, such as a loved one's death by autoerotic asphyxiation (in *World's Greatest Dad*, 2009) and a loved one's experiment with bestiality (in *Sleeping Dogs Lie*, 2006). Compared to those, *Shakes the Clown* is pretty mild, and a quarter century after its release remains the *Citizen Kane* of alcoholic clown movies.

Funny Man (1994)

Funny Man is a ham-handed, low-budget, campy comedy-horror with a steady stream of pop culture references, from *Gremlins* to *The Shining* to *The Fabulous Furry Freak Brothers* underground comic. The film, written and directed by Simon Sprackling, tells the story of a coked-up music producer who wins a castle from Callum Chance (Christopher Lee) in a high-stakes poker game, only to find out that it's haunted by a mischievous and murderous demonic jester called the Funny Man who dispatches his victims one by one, often with sight gags and puns. His antics are similar to those of Killjoy, Freddy Kreuger, and others. The film includes a tarot-reading, Afro-sporting hippie; a ringer for Scooby-Doo's Velma (named Thelma Fudd); and others who fill in the roster of victims.

Funny Man is of particular interest because of the title character's unmistakable roots in Mr. Punch—perhaps not surprising since it's a British production. This evil clown is a scaled-up version of Mr. Punch, from his hunched back to his hook nose and prominent chin. The Funny Man dispatches one woman with a huge bat in classic Punchian procedure, and as her blood spatters the room he turns to the camera and cackles, "Now that *is* the way to do it!" Later in the film we see the Funny Man on an English beach watching a Punch and Judy show in which the head of one of his victims appears on the stage. He is soon decapitated by a bomb (conveniently labeled "bomb," in typical British humor).

To give you some idea of the film's ribald tone, David Endley, production designer for *Funny Man*, noted in the film's commentary that when difficulties plagued the set, it was important for "a transvestite midget from Wales with rubber tits to step in and make it work—and he did!" Though cross-dressing, rubber-titted Welsh dwarves are not typical features of a Christopher Lee film, the veteran actor agreed to do the project because the script was such a departure from his previous work.

Killjoy Series (2000–Present)

Given the popularity of both scary clowns and serial killer franchises (*Friday the Thirteenth, Halloween, A Nightmare on Elm Street,* and so on), it was inevitable that the genres would join and a serial killer clown series would emerge. That happened in 2000 when Full Moon Features studios, long known for B-movie horror films, released a film called *Killjoy* about a demonic killer clown of the same name.

Killjoy had a mostly African American cast and a blaxploitation tone (set in an inner-city gangland), and the character is more of a wisecracking horror villain than a scary monster, distributing bad pun-ishment in the vein of the Crypt Keeper (*Tales from the Crypt*) or Freddy Krueger (*A Nightmare on Elm Street*). It spawned several sequels.

Killjoy 2 lived up to the film's name, plagued by a variety of problems ranging from bad sound to wooden acting as it tells the story of juvenile-detention officers who take a group of "urban street kids" (most of whom appear to be in their late twenties) to a rural area, where, for reasons too absurd to explain, one of them conjures the spirit Killjoy. Despite a few clever lines (one Killjoy victim shouts to another, "We need help! We need the Air Force! We need the S1Ws!"—a reference to the pseudo-military group associated with rap group Public Enemy) and references to everything from *The Shining* to Reginald Denny, the film falters.

Killjoy 3 marked a significant improvement to the series as the character is once again summoned, this time with a few circus-themed friends: there's Batty Boop, the sexy succubus Harlequin-like clown; Punchy, a hobo clown with enormous boxing gloves (played by former pro wrestler Al Burke); and Freakshow, a mime with a parasitic twin. The series abandoned scares for a thoroughly campy tone; at one point Killjoy is identified (by a Snow White–like magic mirror, of all things) as "the baddest motherfucking clown of all." In the third film Killjoy is revealed to be a "demon of vengeance" whose main mission—other than cracking wise—is to collect souls. *Killjoy 3* is more rooted in classical theology than the other films; for example one of the characters explains how he's going to bring Killjoy under his power: "What I'm going to do is call Killjoy by his true name, and that will give his power to me" (Killjoy's real name is Furydahn). This belief that demons and devils have specific, true names—and that by learning and invoking those names they can be controlled—is an ancient one also found in Catholicism (for more on this see Owen Davies's *Grimoires: A History of Magic Books*). The Killjoy franchise has continued with *Killjoy Goes to Hell* and others.

House of 1000 Corpses (2003) and The Devil's Rejects (2005)

Though there are many famous scary clowns, former *Fangoria* editor Tony Timpone says one of his favorites is Captain Spaulding, the clown character in the Rob Zombie films *House of 1000 Corpses* and *The Devil's Rejects*. The films center on a dysfunctional family of serial killers, and Spaulding first appears as the owner of a small rural gas station featuring a side museum of freaks and serial killers.[1] Not much is revealed about Captain Spaulding's life in *The Devil's Rejects*—Zombie has stated that he intentionally left the character's connection to the rest of the killers ambiguous—though in this film Spaulding is revealed to be the leader of the clan.

Roger Ebert summarized the plot as "about a depraved family of mass murderers who name themselves after Groucho Marx characters [including Captain Spaulding, played by Sid Haig]." Ebert offered his own take on the horror of Haig's killer clown: "He is a man whose teeth are so bad, they're more frightening than his clown makeup. He plays such a thoroughly disgusting person, indeed, that I was driven to www.sidhaig.com to discover that in real life Sid looks, well, presentable, and even played a judge in Tarantino's *Jackie Brown*. This was a relief to me, because anyone who really looked like Captain Spaulding would send shoppers screaming from the Wal-Mart" (Ebert 2005).

For Timpone, Captain Spaulding's character "was so well done because you had such a great actor in the makeup, Sid Haig was so wonderful and

FIGURE 6.3. Sadistic clown Captain Spaulding announces that he's on "top secret clown business" on a promotional button for the Rob Zombie horror film *The Devil's Rejects* (2005). From the author's collection.

had a way of delivering lines that were both funny and scary at the same time. And his dialogue was so good. Rob Zombie deserves a lot of credit because I think some of his lines were very Tarantino-esque in cleverness and the way Sid Haig delivered them, it was just so memorable, it just brought an extra depth to it in terms of being funny on one hand and in the next second he could be bashing your head" (Timpone 2006).

The Last Circus (2010)

The Last Circus is a Spanish film that takes place in 1937 during the brutal Spanish Civil War, when a circus clown is conscripted midperformance by a passing militia to fight. The reluctant clown is armed with a machete, and as he and his colleagues prepare to kill Fascist soldiers, he is steeled for battle by a colleague: "A clown with a machete. You'll scare the shit out of them!" He indeed does, though despite his valor he is captured and used as a slave laborer until he is trampled to death in front of his son, Javier.

Fast-forward to the mid-1970s, when the war has been over for decades and Javier is trying to make a life for himself. He wants to be a happy clown like his father, but he has seen too much misery and sadness in his life, including his father's tragic death. He is instead a sad clown with a greasepainted frown. He seeks work with a traveling circus, where he's interviewed by a happy clown named Sergio. "Why do you want to be a clown?" Javier is asked. He replies, "Because if I wasn't a clown I'd be a murderer."

Though career advisors typically advise that job applicants avoid suggesting that they seek the position as a safe outlet for their homicidal impulses, it's apparently the answer Sergio was looking for, as he agrees with Javier and hires him on the spot. Javier tries to adapt to his new circus family and coworkers, though Sergio is soon revealed to be an abusive, alcoholic clown who accuses Javier of having an affair with his beautiful girlfriend, Natalie. The film unfolds as a bloody and surreal love triangle between the happy clown, the sad clown, and the classic femme fatale.

According to writer/director Álex de la Iglesia, the idea for "*The Last Circus* originated in this mental image I had of a clown shooting a machine gun. I'd wanted to shoot [that scene] for the longest time. We'd often discussed the possibility of a psycho killer clown" (de la Iglesia 2010). Though marred by several false endings and a scattered, maudlin third act, *The Last Circus* is an impressive and fascinating film, filled with violent clowns, commandeered ice-cream trucks, gothic carnival pathos, and dwarf tossing.

Scary or Die (2012)

A 2012 short-film anthology titled *Scary or Die* featured a film called "Clowned," in which a California man (played by Corbin Bleu) is bitten by an evil clown named Fucko (whose face paint resembles John Wayne Gacy's Pogo) and in lycanthropic fashion slowly becomes a cannibal clown himself. The clown ends up abducting a young boy (his younger brother), and features a scene of the creepy clown stalking schoolchildren in an echo of the phantom-clown scare (see chapter 12).

I asked Michael Emanuel, the director of *Scary or Die,* what drew him to the scary-clown genre: "I really like to play with tone and I thought what if I took a slice out of Kafka's *Metamorphosis,* and layered in some of . . . *The Werewolf* and then a dash of Bozo and absurd humor what

FIGURE 6.4. Poster art for *Scary or Die*, a 2012 anthology featuring the short film *Clowned*. Phase4Films publicity still.

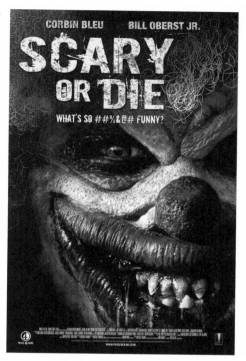

would I have? I wanted to create a horribly sad story about a likable antihero who becomes a monster against his wishes." As for what makes clowns scary, Emanuel says that while he doesn't fear clowns, he definitely hates them. As for why,

> Long story—and not to bring the room down—but a kid who went to my elementary school was John Gacy's first identified victim. Thus the bad clown Fucko is modeled after Gacy's Pogo the Clown. I've always hated clowns but not sure if that hatred came before or after the Gacy incident. Once, as a very young boy, at a local carnival, my cousin snuck me into a freak show. I saw the original Lobster Boy, he was smoking a cigarette and he hocked a huge nasty loogie on the ground near my shoe. I hated him. I hate carnivals and clowns. Mimes too. Fuck, I hate mimes . . . maybe more than clowns. Other than that, I'm a giver.[2] (Emanuel 2014)

Batman (1989) and *The Dark Knight* (2008)

The Joker, perhaps the world's best-known villain and evil clown, was of course a comic-book villain decades before his appearance in film. Yet it was through Hollywood blockbusters that the Joker's image—in portrayals by Jack Nicholson and Heath Ledger in the films (and, to a lesser extent, by Cesar Romero from 1966 to 1968 in the campy television series)— became a global icon.

Coming in fourth in *Entertainment Weekly*'s "Top 20 Villains" in the April 3, 2009, issue (behind the formidable trio of Wicked Witch of the West, Darth Vader, and Hannibal Lecter), the villain, created by Bob Kane, Jerry Robinson, and Bill Finger, was based partly on the character played by Conrad Veidt in the 1928 film *The Man Who Laughs*. Great heroes need great villains, and it's little wonder that Batman's enemy would be powerful and maniacal. "If a hero is only as good as his opponent, then the creation of the Joker cannot be underestimated. 'Villains, I always thought, were more interesting,' [cocreator] Robinson said. He learned from his [Columbia University] studies that some characters were built on their contradictions, so he decided that his evildoer would have a sense of humor. 'I think the name came first: the Joker,' he said. 'Then I thought of the playing card'" (Gustines 2010).

Batman first appeared in 1939 in *Detective Comics* issue 27, though his white-faced archnemesis would make his first appearance the following year in the first issue of *Batman*. The Joker was originally intended to be little more than a single-issue, sadistic serial-killing villain who left a trail of ghastly grinning bodies (the result of his poisonous, proprietary, and patent-pending "Joker Toxin"). However, an editor, sensing the narrative potential of a strong supervillain for Batman, left the door open (and let the comic book end) without the Joker's clear demise. The killer clown's antics were aided, according to *The Essential Batman Encyclopedia*, by

> arrays of gadgets and equipment styled after practical jokes or seemingly innocuous items . . . His boutonniere emitted either deadly gas or acid, while his joy buzzer delivered enough electricity to kill a man. . . . Despite his thin frame, the Joker proved incredibly agile, with tremendous endurance and a high threshold for

pain. He also displayed remarkable strength for a man his size and actually could match Batman blow for blow for brief periods. How he got so strong has not been explained, although it might be a byproduct of the chemical bath that also changed his skin and hair. (Greenberger 2008, 198)

In his book *The Pyrotechnic Insanitarium: American Culture on the Brink*, pop culture critic Mark Dery discusses a psychosocial critique of the Joker:

In the graphic novel *Arkham Asylum*, Batman pays the Joker a visit in the Gotham City sanitarium of the same name. In a wonderful soliloquy that speaks volumes about the ascent of the evil clown in postmodern culture, a psychotherapist explains the Joker's case to his longtime adversary: "We're not even sure if he can be properly defined as insane. . . . It's quite possible we may actually be looking at some kind of super-sanity here. A brilliant new modification of human perception. More suited to urban life at the end of the twentieth century. Unlike you or I, the Joker seems to have no control over the sensory information he's receiving from the outside world. He can only cope with that chaotic barrage of input by going with the flow. That's why some days he's a mischievous clown, other a psychopathic killer. He has no real personality."

The Joker, Dery concludes, is "the man of the hour, perfectly adapted to life in a hall of media mirrors where reality and its fun house double are increasingly indistinguishable" (Dery 1999, 86).

The Joker has undergone many incarnations in the past three-quarters of a century (from Frank Miller's *The Dark Knight Returns* comic miniseries to Tim Burton films to the Mark Hamill–voiced killer clown in *Batman: The Animated Series*), having been played by many actors, having several different origin stories, and so on. A complete discussion of the Joker character—in his countless incarnations and portrayals in books, comics, radio, television, films, graphic novels, and other media—is beyond the scope of this book, but Travis Langley's *Batman and Psychology: A Dark and Stormy Knight* and Matthew Manning's *The Joker: A*

Visual History of the Clown Prince of Crime are good resources. For a discussion of real-life crimes said to have been inspired by the Joker in these Batman films, see chapter 9.

Television Clowns

KRUSTY THE CLOWN (1989 TO PRESENT) AND SIDESHOW BOB (1990 TO PRESENT)

Herschel Shmoikel Pinchas Yerucham Krustofski, better known as Krusty the Clown, is one of the most popular characters on the long-running animated television series *The Simpsons*. On "The Original Krusty the Clown Homepage," a *Simpsons* fan page dedicated to the Krusty character, a contribute writes,

> Krusty's origin is one of the oldest debates here. . . . Who did the writers model Krusty the Clown after? . . . Matt Groening confessed to being mortally afraid of clowns ever since a clown like Krusty humiliated him as a kid. It would be easy, and therefore unrewarding, to make Krusty just the typical 'evil clown' (and would grow old quickly). That's why there's so much more to our favorite clown than meets the eye. Groening revealed that Krusty was based on a local TV clown named Rusty Nails that he used to watch as a kid in Portland. (Sideshow Mike 2009)

FIGURE 6.5. Krusty the Clown figure from *The Simpsons*, manufactured by Re:PLAY Inc., 2000. From the author's collection.

Unlike his incorrigibly homicidal sidekick, Sideshow Bob—who has tried to kill Bart Simpson on multiple occasions—Krusty is not inherently a bad or evil clown.[3] One of the stories told about Krusty was that he was banned from television for saying an expletive (a word too abjectly obscene to reprint here but that is a synonym for *trousers*) live on the air. This is a reference to the famous legend of the foul-mouth incident that was said to have led to Bozo the Clown being banned.

STEPHEN KING'S *It* (1990)

While *Killer Klowns from Outer Space* from 1988 is a camp classic, by far the most memorable scary clown in visual media is evil clown Pennywise in *It*, based on Stephen King's 1986 novel of the same name. Played by Tim Curry, Pennywise (see plate 13) was a murderous evil-incarnate entity capable of transforming itself into whatever form a person most feared. A group of outcasts first encounter Pennywise as teenagers, and then later reunite as adults to defeat him.

It was not a feature film but instead a two-part television miniseries that aired in 1990 on the ABC network. A key reason that evil clown Pennywise is so widely known is that *It* was seen in nearly 18 million households, including by children and teenagers. If *It* had been a PG- or R-rated theatrical release its audience would have been cut by two-thirds. It might (or might not) have been scarier with the addition of a bigger budget, explicit gore, and the profanity likely to accompany a big-screen studio release, but it clearly would not have had the lasting cultural impact that the television production did. Never before had a scary clown appeared in living rooms across the country during prime time.

In a 2013 interview Stephen King explained how Pennywise came to be: "I thought to myself, 'What scares children more than anything else in the world?' And the answer was clowns. So I created Pennywise the Clown in *It*. And then what happened was ABC came along and said they wanted to make a miniseries out of it and they wanted to cast Tim Curry as Pennywise. I thought it was a really strange idea but it really worked, and it scared a whole generation of young people, it made them scared of clowns. Clowns are scary for children to start with" (King 2013).

In a 2005 interview on *Late Night with Conan O'Brien*, Conan O'Brien credited King as "one of the first people to have the idea that a clown could be a scary figure." He asked King if he'd been scared of clowns as a child, and King replied with his own early experience: "As a kid going to the circus, there would be like twelve full grown people that would all pile out of a little tiny car, their faces were dead white, their mouths were red as though they were full of blood. They're all screaming, their eyes are huge. . . . What's not to like?"

King gently corrected O'Brien, noting that he hardly invented the scary-clown idea, though he certainly popularized it for many around the world. "So I started to actually look at kids. . . . Kids are all terrified of them. The parents are like, 'Aren't the clowns funny, Johnny?' and Johnny's like, 'No! Get me the hell out of here! These people are all crazy!' because they really are monstrous looking and children are all afraid of them, they do sort of have that monstrous thing going for them."

Though King himself admitted no particular fear of clowns, he told a (perhaps apocryphal) story of a strange clown he encountered on an airplane early in his career:

> It was my first big book tour, I was on my way home . . . and the plane pulls away from the gate, and then it pulls back in. I'm sitting in first class, and the door opens again, and Ronald McDonald gets on the airplane. He's fully dressed, and sits down next to me—because I attract weirdness, I'm like a weirdness magnet. And I was so weirded out by that point [from a long, exhausting book tour including] rubber chicken dinners that I wasn't even surprised. Here he is, orange hair, orange shoes, the whole nine yards. He sits down next to me—this is years ago—the plane takes off, the 'no smoking' light goes off, he pulls out a pack of Kents, lights up a Kent, and he orders a gin and tonic from the stewardess. . . . He had come from McDonaldland, which is a real place in Chicago, and he was going to open a McDonald's in Burlington, Vermont. You talk about surreal, and I thought, "What if this plane crashes? I'm going to die next to a clown." (King 2005)

According to Tony Timpone,

Originally Pennywise was going to be [created with] really elaborate makeup. The director, Tommy Lee Wallace, told me they had a series of makeups for Pennywise, where he gets more and more over-the-top-scary looking, and Tim Curry said "You know, I don't want to go through all the makeup, I want to be able to act. I think I can make this character scary with a minimal amount of makeup," and I think that was a wise decision because Curry was such a good actor, he knows how to handle the language, he made the character exceptionally scary just by using simple greasepaint, his body language, and that funny, menacing voice. (Timpone 2006)

Curry's performance became indelibly linked to scary clowns everywhere and years later inspired copycat clowns such as the Northampton and Staten Island Clowns (see chapter 9).

Despite occasional premature proclamations of retirement, Stephen King continues to write best sellers well into the new century, but for many he will forever be most closely associated with the evil clown he first introduced in 1986. A theatrical version of *It* began filming in 2015 and is slated for a 2016 release.

YUCKO THE CLOWN

One of the most popular bad clowns of the late 1990s was a bald-capped madcap clown named Yucko (see plate 14). According to his semiofficial biography,

Yucko the Clown was born on Christmas Day, 1952 in Coney Island, New York to a family of gypsy immigrants. His father was a one-legged midget hermaphrodite who worked at a meat packing plant. His mother was a chain-smoking prostitute who sold her wares to help raise Yucko and his mentally retarded brother Clovis. Yucko grew up on the boardwalk, selling cotton candy and hot dogs and started drinking at age 10. After many run-ins with the law, Yucko finally joined the circus and began a three-year affair with the bearded lady. Eventually he was fired for solicitation of a circus elephant and was sentenced to five years on Ryker's [*sic*] Island. He was paroled and moved south to do his act on the streets for tips and liquor. (*Damn! Show* 2005)

With an upbringing like that, it's not surprising that "Yucko the Clown" achieved attention and eventually became part of the [Howard Stern show] Wack Pack by running onto the field during a major league baseball game while carrying a Howard Stern sign. Sporting the traditional clown outfit and makeup, Yucko is an angry, nasty clown spewing a never-ending rant filled with insults and curses. . . . Away from the Wack Pack, Yucko has his own following and has appeared on MTV's Stankervision and Jimmy Kimmel's talk show. He also has a Web site from which he sells his own DVDs" (Mintzer 2010, 87).

With a microphone in one hand and a bicycle horn in the other, Yucko wanders around with a camera crew looking for victims. Yucko's shtick varies, though his most prominent sketches involve him doing clown-on-the-street interviews with passersby in places such as New York's Times Square, New Orleans's Bourbon Street, and at Utah's Sundance Film Festival. His antics appeared on a television series called *The Damn! Show.*

Yucko is—or pretends to be—inebriated during his interviews, sometimes slurring words and offering lewd questions seemingly hatched in a haze borne of cut-rate bourbon. The banter ranges from the scatological to the profane and is often in the vein, not surprisingly, of insult humor. Though some of Yucko's banter is witty, much of it relies on shock value; for example when Yucko greets a woman who is wearing a typical balloon-animal hat, he wittily informs her, "You look fuckin' stupid!" Other common targets of Yucko's abuse are teeth, breasts, and ethnic minorities. Though passersby are often targets of Yucko's harassment, street performers and homeless people are sometimes included for variety.

Yucko also branched out into doing prank phone calls, joining a mid-1990s fad perhaps best exemplified by Queens-based comedy duo the Jerky Boys, who called unsuspecting restaurants, doctors, and other businesses with bizarre complaints and non sequiturs. Yucko's 2008 offering, titled "Yucko the Clown: Eat My Balls!" was critically snubbed and failed to receive a single Grammy nomination.

Yucko is essentially an insult comic dressed as a clown (instead of, for example, a clown who insults people), though he borrows several clown props such as an annoying bicycle horn and several nonclown props such as a dildo. Another of Yucko's signatures is a manic little dance in which he slaps his feet down in place as if working himself into a berserker rage or trying to dislodge a short-circuiting 9-volt battery "accidentally" left in his perineum.

Yucko the Clown wears a red nose, garish red makeup around his mouth, and white face paint. His bald cap is bullet headed and tellingly phallic, with exaggerated eyebrow lines and a fringe of green hair. Yucko's costume is intentionally dirty and foul. Roger Black, Yucko's alter ego, retired the character in September 2013 on the *Howard Stern Show*. Black removed his wig live on *Howard TV*, (apparently) ending his appearances as Yucko. Black took the opportunity to promote his latest endeavor, a Comedy Central show called *Brickleberry*. Stern wished his former Wack Pack member well and expressed some skepticism that Yucko was gone for good: "I don't know how much of a retirement this is. I think if things go shitty again in Roger's life, Yucko's coming right out of the closet." Indeed, the Yucko character, though not making as many prominent public appearances as when he was on *The Damn! Show*, remained active on Twitter as of 2015. In a typical tweet in April 2014 Yucko the Clown helpfully updated his thirty-four thousand followers who might have been curious about his aromatic status: "I smell like warm dog shit."

HOMEY D. CLOWN

The 1990–1994 Fox-network sitcom *In Living Color* featured a character named Herman Simpson, better known as Homey D. Clown. The skits typically followed a formulaic narrative in which (adults playing) children at a party are delighted to hear that a clown has arrived, until they get the feeling that something isn't right in the head with this particular bitter clown. Homey uses a horn and a sock full of coins to beat and terrorize the tykes. Homey, an African American clown, has a pathological aversion to playing the fool, informed by an indignant, race-conscious sensibility. Homey works out his frustrations about what he considers to be racist encounters with "The Man" (invariably white), in which he is rejected.

Homey attributes any perceived rejection or mistreatment as caused by racism (as opposed to him showing up at a fancy restaurant being dressed as a clown, for example).

When asked to perform typical clown routines and antics, Homey replies, "So I can degrade and shame myself for your amusement. You'd like that, wouldn't you?" followed by the signature line and a Mr. Punch–inspired smack: "Homey don't play dat!" He dispenses abuse and degradation to one or more of the children and makes his position clear: "Let's get something straight, kids: Homey may be a clown, but he don't make a fool outa hisself." When asked by one of the children why he became a clown, Homey responds in one episode, "I guess it's because I got so much love to give," then adds, "And it's part of my prison work-release program. I got about five more years of this clown crap." Homey's image and catchphrase was enormously popular in the early 1990s, appearing on T-shirts, mugs, and other merchandise.

BOZO'S BALL-BUSTING BUFFOONERY

When it comes to bad behavior and real television clowns, one story stands a full fluorescent fright wig above them all. It's the story of the time Bozo the Clown and a young boy exchanged harsh words live on the air in front of millions of impressionable children on Bozo's show during the 1950s.

Various versions of this story have circulated for decades. In his book *Truth and Rumors: The Reality Behind TV's Most Famous Myths*, Bill Brioux explains that

> Bozo the Clown was the McDonald's of children's television. . . . Created to promote a series of Capitol records back in the 1940s, Bozo became a TV property in the mid-1950s when entrepreneur Larry Harmon bought the rights to "The World's Most Famous Clown." . . . Suddenly there were Bozos from Green Bay to Baton Rouge. But it was in Boston where Bozo really got under some kid's skin. Harmon told the story to *TV Guide* in 1998. The clown was working a live show on Boston's now defunct WCVB. It was a show Harmon happened to be producing. It was during [a segment called] Bozo's Treasure Chest—a kiddie toy grab contest—that Junior blew

his stack. Harmon says it was some "young, underprivileged kid" with "eyes as big as saucers looking at these toys" who was *this* close to winning a prize when he missed the third and last question. The show's ringmaster tells the kid, "You're never a loser on the Bozo show, you're just an almost-winner," and handed the kid a crummy Bozo towel. To which Junior replied, "Cram it, clown." "That's a Bozo no-no," was apparently the clown's live and speedy response. (Brioux 2008, 130)

It's a funny and plausible story—after all, kids say the darndest things; there were such games and contests on the Bozo show; and it's certain that at least a few of the snot-nosed tykes were not good sports when they lost.[4] And of course there is always a risk of something unexpected or embarrassing happening during any live broadcast, from U2's Bono saying "fucking brilliant" while onstage during the Golden Globe Awards in 2003 to Janet Jackson exposing her nipple during a half-time performance at the Super Bowl a year later.

But is this story true? Many people in addition to Brioux claim it is, though no source is given and he seems to rely entirely on Harmon's anecdote. Folklore experts, however, are skeptical. In his book *The Truth Never Stands in the Way of a Good Story*, urban-legend researcher Jan Harold Brunvand devotes an extensive chapter to examining this story. He notes that

"Bozo the Clown's Blooper" is not one story, really, but two. . . . The first version of the story focuses on a child who is a contestant on a local Bozo the Clown TV program. The child misses a shot in a game of dexterity and utters a curse. When Bozo attempts to comfort him, the child snaps, in the most common version, "Cram it, clown!" The outburst goes out over the airwaves, shocking the clown's young audience—and no doubt the parents too. In the second version of the story, the offensive words are uttered by Bozo himself. The clown, exasperated by his young contestants, calls one of them an unprintable name. The comment goes out over the air, and irate parents call the TV station in protest. Before long the local Bozo the Clown show is canceled.

As for whether the first version of the legend is true or not,

> former Bozo actors and agents deny that the story of the child's
> naughty remark is true, and the many variations I've heard support
> them. I've heard the story told about the Bozos of Baltimore, New
> Orleans, Chicago, and Los Angeles; I've heard that Bozo called the
> child's remark a "Bozo no-no"; and I've heard that the kid said "ram
> it" or "shove it" or "climb it" instead of "cram it." I've been told that
> the child made an obscene gesture and said much naughtier words—
> the f-word, even—as well as "Screw you, Bozo!" and "Eat shit,
> Bozo!" I've heard that the child was playing a ball-in-bucket game, a
> block-building contest, an egg-in-spoon game, or was taking part in a
> quiz game. (Brunvand 2000, 85)

Obviously not all these stories can be true, despite people swearing up
and down that a friend of a friend was in the studio that day, or saw it
live at home. In fact there is no evidence that the story is anything more
than an entertaining urban legend, a famous clown embarrassed on his
own show by a mouthy kid.

The history of the second version—the one involving the world's most
famous clown uttering a profanity at an annoying and shocked child—
is a little more complicated. That incident was actually first attributed to
a different children's show host, who wasn't even a clown. Brunvand
writes,

> [I]t is very likely that the version of the 'Bozo the Clown's Blooper'
> legend . . . was transferred to Bozo the Clown from an event
> attributed to the early children's radio show host who called himself
> Uncle Don. This alleged radio incident, however, is debunked in
> every available reference work on broadcasting history. . . . The
> legend about the radio show cussing the kids, in fact, was being told
> concerning at least one other broadcaster at about the same time
> that Uncle Don was enjoying his greatest success. It was probably a
> standard story told to illustrate the hazards of live radio in the early
> days. (Brunvand 2000, 88)

In their book *Rumor!* Hal Morgan and Kerry Tucker (1984) note that a Bozo-free version of the rumor spread in the 1960s claimed that "a children's television show host was taken off the air after he said, 'That ought to shut the little bastards up!' on live television during what he thought was a commercial break" (Morgan and Tucker 1984, 92–93).

Thus it's a story widely repeated and attributed to many kid's-show hosts, and one that probably never even happened. It's not hard to fathom why the version associated with Bozo the Clown is the only one that remains in the public's consciousness today: it highlights the ironic contrast between the wholesome clown and what happens in real life. In the end, when all the sawdust has settled it seems that Bozo and a child on his show did not tell each other off on live television, or any other time. Even if Bozo didn't say it, he probably should have.

Other Bad Clowns

Other notable bad clowns appear in *S.I.C.K. Serial Insane Clown Killer* (2003), *Klown Kamp Massacre* (2010), *Camp Blood* (1999), *Sloppy the Psychotic* (2012), *Clown* (2014), and *Clownhouse* (1989). *Fear of Clowns*, a 2007 B-movie features Shivers, an axe-wielding clown tormenting a coulrophobic artist. In the director commentary for the film, writer/director Kevin Kangas gives his take on why people fear clowns: "Masked people are scary, and really, what is a clown besides somebody with a painted-on mask?" *Blood Harvest* is a bizarre 1987 film featuring Tiny Tim as a creepy clown named Mervo who may or may not be stalking a young woman on a rural farm.

An evil clownlike puppet can be found in the *Saw* horror-film franchise. It has the appearance of a white-faced clown, with blood-red spiral circles on his cheeks. Though never named in the series, he is referred to informally as Billy the Puppet and was used as the face of the sadistic serial killer and torturer John Kramer, better known as Jigsaw.

Another honorable bad-clown mention goes to an excellent 2003 short documentary film by David Manning titled *Clowns at War*, revealing a little-known but highly effective "clown brigade" that helped defeat the Nazis during World War II. As of 2015 the film could be found on YouTube at https://www.youtube.com/watch?v=h95eWMmesOo.

Around Halloween 2014, the acclaimed FX cable TV series *American Horror Story* launched its fourth season, titled *Freak Show*, with a circus and carnival theme—including a truly terrifying clown named Twisty. According to a story in the *Hollywood Reporter*,

> Real clowns see nothing funny about their depiction in *American Horror Story: Freak Show*. The FX series from Ryan Murphy and Brad Falchuk revolves around Twisty the Clown (John Carroll Lynch), a serial killer who stalks couples with scissors and imprisons children in an old school bus. "Hollywood makes money sensationalizing the norm," bemoans Glenn Kohlberger, president of Clowns of America International, the nation's biggest clown club. "They can take any situation no matter how good or pure and turn it into a nightmare. We do not support in any way, shape or form any medium that sensationalizes or adds to coulrophobia or 'clown fear.'" (Abramovich 2014)

Some see the bad clown persona in nonclown film characters. Mark Dery, for example, views the lead character in *The Shining* as a form of evil clown:

> [Jack] Nicholson's Torrance is an evil clown, emblematizing the off-the-rails, media-giddy mind-set of America late in the twentieth century. Appropriately, pop culture has embraced him as a gonzo anti-hero: ads for T-shirts emblazoned with the "Here's Johnny" Nicholson, all wild eyes and vulpine smile, have been a fixture on the back pages of magazines like *Rolling Stone* for some time now. . . . We've seen it before, or variations on it, on the faces that float in the darkness of our collective dreams: Robert DeNiro as Travis Bickle, the walking time bomb with the dorky grin in *Taxi Driver*; Woody Harrelson as Mickey Knox, the mad-dog killer with the twinkle in his eye in *Natural Born Killers*; Michael Madsen as Vic Vega, the smirking psychopath in *Reservoir Dogs*, who tortures a cop "not to get information, but because torturing a cop amuses me." (Dery 1999, 80–81)

There's some truth to this, though surely not every wisecracking sadist or pop culture–referencing psychopath who carries out his or her duties with anything but single-minded solemnity is a clown figure.

On the nonfiction-film side, Peter J. Haskett, the verbally abusive alcoholic whose alternately (and infamously) foul and funny 1990s tirades against his gay roommate Raymond were captured on audiotape and seen in the 2010 documentary *Shut Up, Little Man! An Audio Misadventure* is certainly a candidate for an evil-clown character. A website offering the audio describes the content: "The Shut Up Little Man recordings feature the real-life comical rants, hateful harangues, drunken soliloquies, and audible fistfights of Raymond and Peter, two booze-swilling homicidal roommates in a low-rent district of San Francisco. These infamous recordings were made by their much-menaced next-door neighbors, Eddie Lee and Mitchell D. The dialogs of Raymond and Peter have been widely championed for their poignant absurdity and stark hilarity" (Shut Up Little Man LLC 2008). In hours of clandestinely recorded fights, the pair hurl surreal threats, invective, and non sequiturs at each other such as "You always giggle falsely. You don't have a decent giggle in you!" and "I can kill you from a sitting position." Haskett as evil clown is particularly interesting because he doesn't appear to be making any attempt at humor in his abuse and (empty) threats; the comedy derives from the absurdity of his comments and the profoundly twisted nature of their relationship.

CHAPTER 7

Bad Clowns of the Song

Though bad clowns are prominent in visual and printed media, music has had its share of dubious clowns. Here is a brief look at some prominent bad clowns from the music world. The band Acid Bath issued an album featuring several pieces of art by serial killer John Wayne Gacy, including a self-portrait of himself performing as Pogo the Clown (see chapter 9).

Wall of Voodoo Clowns

The 1980s New Wave group Wall of Voodoo provided some of the most memorable bad clowns in rock music. They appear on two albums, first on *Seven Days in Sammystown* (1985). In the music video for the song on that album titled "Far Side of Crazy," the band—fronted by lead singer Andy Prieboy—travels through the desert in a car until they come across a clown sitting alone. Upon seeing them he immediately picks up a camcorder and begins filming them as they approach. The clown later reappears in a room, handing Prieboy what appears to be a heart-shaped box of chocolates. Prieboy accepts it, but upon opening it finds it contains cockroaches. It's perhaps a metaphor for false promises and disillusionment.

FIGURE 7.1. Poster for the 1985 Wall of Voodoo album *Seven Days in Sammystown.* From the author's collection.

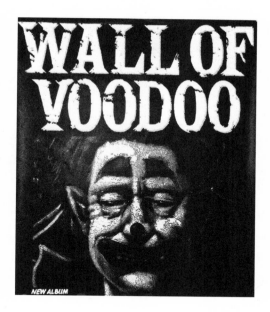

SEVEN DAYS IN SAMMYSTOWN

I contacted Prieboy and asked him about the significance of bad and disgruntled clown themes in Wall of Voodoo's music and tone of that era. "When I was invited to join Voodoo, the Hollywood of 1984 was that of 1932 on its deathbed. It still looked like the charming Hollywood Boulevard of Bogie and Harold Lloyd—only dirty, populated by the homeless, runaways, the insane, whores, hop heads, needle freaks, and various sex and music or art groups. And tourists," he added. "Idiotic, clueless, trusting tourists." The Los Angeles–based band had close ties to Las Vegas:

The guys of Voodoo were hard-line gamblers and drinkers. Vegas was their Rome. And at the time Vegas was like a dying Mafioso, tawdry and tacky. In 1984, Vegas was a thing of the past, it had been so for a long time. Before our Corporate Insect Masters breathed new life into it Vegas was a place for incurable gamblers and squares only. The 1980s Vegas was the 1950s Vegas gasping for air. The guys in Voodoo saw themselves in these desperate grasps at booze and easy money. So there was a tie in between these two spiritual centers, Vegas and Hollywood. The music industry was like playing the slots:

any idiot can do well. And, like Vegas, the people who ran the music industry were cheap thugs. They sold dreams to pie-eyed tourists, the rubes and idealists.

So when the black velvet clown [on the cover of *Sammystown*] found us, he made sense. [Wall of Voodoo bandmates] Chas [Gray] and Marc and Bruce [Moreland] had started out as punk rock idealists. A few years as professional recording and touring musicians had destroyed their illusions. The good intentions had soured, the inner rot had blistered and popped. The showbiz smile was painted on and underneath an exhausted grimace of yellowed teeth. (Prieboy 2014)

With this emotional and mental image in the band's collective consciousness, the group had recorded an album of material that, as yet, had neither a title nor a cover.

At the time, there was a billboard in Vegas that featured the Mr. Punch-like mug of Sammy Davis Jr.—*Welcome to Sammy's Town!* it said. There was our title: Sammystown, a hybrid of both shitholes. With that in mind, we were kicking around ideas for a tawdry look of cheap glamor for the album cover. Someone suggested a black velvet painting and we all agreed. I suggested it be flocked and thus offer a classy *imitation* black velvet painting—even better. Marc and Chas wanted a black velvet landscape, with Las Vegas in the distance with all its glittering, promising glory. An artist they liked was hired. A few weeks later it was done, and we were all on hand for the unveiling. I hated it. IRS Records president Miles Copeland hated it. There was no contrast, like a good black velvet painting has. If it had been reduced to an ad in newsprint, it would have looked like a slice of lasagna. This was not received well by the other members of Wall of Voodoo. I, as the new guy [following the departure of Stan Ridgway], had overstepped my bounds—and worse, agreed with the label president. . . . We searched all over L.A. for a black velvet painting that in some way inferred our title, *Seven Days in Sammystown,*

but nothing could be found.

The relationship between the band and their record label was volatile at the best of times, and the whole thing exploded when Copeland insisted that Voodoo do a support tour for Adam Ant. The move was intended to introduce *Sammystown* and the band's new lineup to the public, but it proved to be a fateful spark. Long-simmering annoyances and resentments erupted; one of the members quit Wall of Voodoo and vanished; robust screaming matches ensued between the record label, management, and band, draining everyone and souring relationships.

Finally, Prieboy recalls,

Marc invited us to his apartment to talk. Chas and I arrived and Marc's girlfriend invited us in. Marc was out getting cigarettes. We sat in the living room exhausted. We lit cigarettes. And waited. I casually mentioned that I had still to find a proper image for the album cover. Exasperated, Chas said "Fuck it. Album covers don't sell albums!" He pointed a cigarette at a black velvet happy clown painting Marc had on the mantle. "We could use that stupid fucking clown for an album cover, for all it really fucking matters." I jumped up: "That's it! That's it!" I shouted. I stood in front of it, pointing at the clown. "We make his skin like an Albright painting . . . like an Albright black velvet painting!" With my fingernails, I added an outline of a Gin Lane behind him. For years after, you could see where my fingers had made their marks.

That night Prieboy made a series of cover mockups using black paper and chalk. A few days later most of the band's differences had been tolerably resolved in time for a meeting with the label president. "He turned me and said, 'Let's talk about the album cover.' I opened my portfolio and showed them my sketches. The entire room erupted in laughter at the sight of a sick, hungover clown on skid row." The clown perfectly symbolized not only the album's gritty, grotty themes but also the band's inner turmoil and disillusionment.

Disgruntled clowns also made an appearance in Wall of Voodoo's 1988 live album *The Ugly Americans in Australia*. The album cover, painted by Robert Williams, has several popular titles including *Two-Fisted Buffoons* and *Dueling Bimbos*, though its museum catalog title is *An*

Allegory Of Contradictions Revealing Serendipity Purveyors Of Mirth Presenting A Tableau Of Blood And Greasepaint In A Circusian Clash To The Death (see plate 16). It's not clear what, exactly, the two, two-fisted buffoons are fighting over. It could be over the affections of the scantily clad Siamese twins watching in horror; or perhaps one of the clowns is responsible for the flames licking at the circus tent in the background. Those with knowledge of clown lore may find another possible bone of contention in the scene: the clowns are wearing similar makeup, and copying another clown's makeup is strictly verboten—the circusian equivalent of fightin' words. It could be that one or the other felt that the other's makeup was too similar to his own and thus his clowny honor was in need of defense.

The Ugly Americans would be the final studio album for Wall of Voodoo, fulfilling their contractual obligations to IRS Records, and the group disbanded the following year. Andy Prieboy continues to make music, and the evil clown theme has reappeared in his solo work. The cover artwork for his 1991 EP *Montezuma Was a Man of Faith*, for example, features a striking stained glass piece by Judith Schaechter titled *Rape Serenade* of a clown attacking a woman. His 2010 release *The Questionable Profits of Pure Novelty* has yet another clown on the cover, though this one catches the circus fat lady wounded in a riot. Perhaps Prieboy's clown has awoken from his self-destructive delirium, developing a sense of empathy along the way. Or maybe he's just using the fat lady as a shield.

Another Los Angeles–based musician, singer-songwriter Warren Zevon, best known for his lyrics about memorable scoundrels in songs such as Roland the Headless Thompson Gunner, Werewolves of London, and Excitable Boy, also wrote a song about clowns. In a song from his 1995 album *Mutineer* titled "Something Bad Happened to a Clown," he sings of a clown who used to don his red nose and his squirting flower, honking his horn for the adoring crowds. An unidentified woman in the song decided he wasn't funny anymore, and Zevon sings dolefully of "footprints in the sawdust leading to the edge of town." The fate of the song's once-mirthful clown remains unknown—other than that something decidedly bad happened to him. And it was probably not painless.

Insane Clown Posse and Juggalos

In the world of hip-hop music the best-known clowns are also the most infamous ones: Violent J and Shaggy 2 Dope, the clown-clad duo comprising the horrorcore (a rap/metal fusion genre) group Insane Clown Posse. Their stylized logo is a silhouette (seemingly of a crazed clown) running with a meat cleaver.

They have released about a dozen studio albums since their formation in 1989. Their song lyrics often contain depictions of graphic murder, drug deals, violent revenge, and so on. This theme is of course not new; in 1955 country music legend Johnny Cash sang that he "shot a man in Reno just to watch him die," and thirty years later gangster rappers such as Ice-T and the members of NWA would sing first-person songs about killings and street vengeance. The difference is that this time it's popular clowns singing the songs.

Fans of Insane Clown Posse, called Juggalos, have been labeled a criminal organization. A 2011 report from the National Gang Intelligence Center, part of the Federal Bureau of Investigation, identified Juggalos as a violent gang. The report reads in part,

> The Juggalos, a loosely-organized hybrid gang, are rapidly expanding into many U.S. communities. Although recognized as a gang in only four states [Arizona, California, Pennsylvania, and Utah], many Juggalos subsets exhibit gang-like behavior and engage in criminal activity and violence. Law enforcement officials in at least 21 states have identified criminal Juggalo sub-sets. . . . Most crimes committed by Juggalos are sporadic, disorganized, individualistic, and often involve simple assault, personal drug use and possession, petty theft, and vandalism. However, open source reporting suggests that a small number of Juggalos are forming more organized subsets and engaging in more gang-like criminal activity, such as felony assaults, thefts, robberies, and drug sales. Social networking websites are a popular conveyance for Juggalo sub-culture to communicate and expand. (National Gang Intelligence Center 2011, 12)

The National Gang Intelligence Center argument seemed to be that—

like magnets (however they work)—Juggalos inevitably attract crime. As evidence of their inherent criminal tendencies, the report notes that "in January 2011, a suspected Juggalo member shot and wounded a couple in King County, Washington," and a year before that "two suspected Juggalo associates were charged with beating and robbing an elderly homeless man." Just to drive the point home—and in an effort to make the Juggalos seem as dangerous as possible—the report includes a photo of face-painted Juggalette pointing a gun.

The premise underlying the supposed culture of violence in the Juggalo community rested on a handful of "suspected" Juggalos who were charged with committing violent crimes. Out of the tens of thousands of Juggalos around the word, and the millions of people who regularly listen to the music of Insane Clown Posse but do not self-identify as hardcore Juggalos, there have been a few who have committed serious crimes. Records are of course not kept of the number of crimes committed by fans of other musical groups—asking a suspect's favorite music is not standard police booking procedure—thus there's no way to know how many fans of Ronnie James Dio, Neil Diamond, or Katy Perry may have also committed similar crimes (or been suspected of them).

Under what definition might Juggalos qualify as a criminal "street gang"? Well, Title 18 U.S.C. Section 521(a)(A) defines "'criminal street gang' [as] an ongoing group, club, organization, or association of 5 or more persons . . . that has as 1 of its primary purposes the commission of 1 or more criminal offenses." Using this broad a definition, it's hardly surprising that a group of five or more Juggalos somewhere might join up to commit a crime, but tarring all Juggalos as *de facto* criminals paints with a broad brush indeed. In early 2014 Insane Clown Posse, with the assistance of the American Civil Liberties Union, filed a lawsuit against the FBI challenging its designation of their fans as criminals. It was dismissed by a federal judge in July 2014, who ruled that the FBI's designation of Juggalos as a gang was descriptive, not prescriptive—that is, the music fans could technically be described as a gang under Title 18 definitions, but the FBI report did not state that all Juggalos were by definition criminals or gang members (Ohlheiser 2014).

According to British author Jon Ronson, writing for the *Guardian* in 2010, Insane Clown Posse, despite a notorious reputation for its over-

FIGURE 7.2. An evil, blood-spattered clown uses children as marionettes on the poster for the 2015 tour of the Spanish band Mägo de Oz. Purchased in Baños, Ecuador, in April 2015, from the author's collection.

the-top songs about violence and misogyny that's gotten them banned (for example, from Canada because of the members' criminal records, and from an Albuquerque, New Mexico, venue following a riot), is actually a devoutly Christian group. Ronson noted that "Insane Clown Posse have this entire time secretly been evangelical Christians. They've only been pretending to be brutal and sadistic to trick their fans into believing in God. . . . While some fans claimed they'd actually had an inkling, having deciphered some of the hidden messages in several songs, others said they felt deeply betrayed and outraged: they'd been innocently enjoying all those songs about chopping people up and shooting women, and it was Christian rock?" (Ronson 2010). Regardless of whether Insane Clown Posse promotes violence or subtly denounces it through clever satire, their legacy in the history of evil clowns is undeniable.

Following a similar trajectory, the Spanish folk / heavy metal band Mägo de Oz (Wizard of Oz) recently featured a bad clown on their promotional posters for the band's 2015 "Ilussia 3D" tour. A menacing clown with a blood-spattered face and fanged teeth holds two life-like marionette children while freaks and phalluses fire cannons in the background.

Rap's Public Enemy Clown: Flavor Flav

Flavor Flav is a prominent member of the political and pioneering rap group Public Enemy and one of rap music's best-known bad clowns. Flavor Flav's clownlike taunts and calls (including "Yeah Boyeee!") are only part of the package; he's no ordinary clown, and he has a fashion style all his own. His clownlike props include oversized hats, striking Viking helmets, gold crowns, top hats (both black and white), baseball caps positioned in a topologically exhaustive variety of positions on his head, purple satin shirts, and a dizzying array of clocks. And, of course, there are the gold chains, gaudy rings, and gold teeth that spell out his name when he smiles.

In a playing-card set issued by the British magazine *New Musical Express* Flavor Flav appears, quite appropriately, as the Joker of the deck. He's the flavor, the chaotic, clownish spark plug who serves as a comic relief to straight man Chuck D, the "juice man" who calls 911 "a joke" and makes up his own nonsensical words. In his book *Funk: The Music, the People, and the Rhythm of the One*, author Rickey Vincent discusses Flav's key role in Public Enemy:

> What was crucial to the partnership, it should be noted, is that Flavor Flav was a clown—in the tradition of the best black comics— yet he was a clown with consciousness, empowered with knowledge of self, an entirely different persona from the "Stepin Fetchit" and "Sambo" stereotypes of subservient and uncouth black Americans. Flavor Flav was and is a fool, but a fool on a mission. On the cover of [the 1988 album *It Takes A Nation of Millions to Hold Us Back*] he wears a gigantic clock as a medallion—a preposterous getup—yet it is designed to illustrate, through a comic medium, that time is indeed running out. (Vincent 1996)

Entertainment Weekly writer Margeaux Watson deemed Flavor Flav's large clock-as-necklace fashion fad "regrettable," but it fit in perfectly with the historical role of the clown as truth teller. His signature callout references the clock around his neck: "What time is it?" In rap lexicon, time is a universal, understood truth. If someone doesn't know "what

FIGURE 7.3. Flavor Flav as
the Joker in a deck of playing
cards issued by *New Musical
Express*. From the author's
collection.

time it is," as rappers such as Flavor Flav and Eazy-E have accused others, it means they don't know the essential truth of what's going on. Another favorite Flavor phrase is the classic skeptical mantra "Don't believe the hype."

The clock may have started out as joke but Flav said it eventually served a more serious purpose. In a 1994 interview for MTV, Flav explained the significance of the clock:

> The reason why I wear this clock is because you know, it represents time, you know what I'm sayin', as being the most important element in our life, you know what I'm sayin'. Time can't afford to be wasted, you know what I'm sayin'. And not only that, but you know, God only gave us one life, you know what I'm sayin'. So each minute we live, we got to live each second to our best value, you know what I'm sayin'. Time brought us in here, and time can also take us out, you know what I'm sayin'. I always say, 'I'm clockin,' I'm clockin'. That means I'm paying attention, so you can't get fast on me because I know what time it is! (MTV 2009)

This is, of course, an updated version of Benjamin Franklin's carpe diem admonition: "Do you love life? Then waste not time, for time is the stuff of life."

Like many clowns before him, Flav has battled demons who have at times bested him. According to Flav, "I was battling drug addiction. I had just introduced myself to crack and cocaine. The devil turned me on to that shit. That's who I was [hanging out] with—the devil. . . . Quaaludes, angel dust, PCP, cocaine, crack, alcohol, weed—your boy did it all back in the days" (quoted in Watson 2006). In 1991 the drug use added fuel to the fire, and he was arrested for domestic violence against his girlfriend. He lost custody of his children and had intermittent brushes with the law. As of 2014 Flavor Flav continues to tour and perform with Public Enemy, though in recent years his reality-TV presence has overshadowed his musical clowning antics.

CHAPTER 8

The Carnal Carnival

Buffoon Boffing and Clown Sex

The subjects of clown sex and pornography have received relatively little attention in the hallowed halls and ivory towers of academia; whether out of prudery, good judgment, or merely a discomfort with the images that would be required for a scholarly PowerPoint on the topic at a conference among respected peers, the topic has largely been ignored.

Clowns having sex is not, of course, inherently bad or evil, and therefore it stands to reason that photographs, videos, films, and other depictions of copulating clowns is also not inherently bad. Clowns are, after all, invariably past the age of consent (child clowns are virtually unheard of, clowning being an adult occupation), and whatever makes a consenting clown's nose glow red in the privacy of his or her trailer is a private matter.

Nonetheless it's not surprising that many people are unnerved by clown porn. Even though many versions of the clown have traditionally been performed for adult audiences and did not shy away from working blue, modern clowns are often associated with children, children's parties, and circuses—none of which serve as sources of arousal for normal people, especially when coupled with the widespread dislike of clowns. Cara Bruce, a San Francisco–based editor, author, and coauthor of several books of erotica, including *Tarnished: True Tales of Innocence Lost, Best Bisexual Women's Erotica*, and *Best Fetish Erotica*, notes that "clown porn does exist and so do clown fetishists. . . . Is it the uniform, or costume, that makes this group ripe for fetishism? Or is it the taboo factor? Clowns are associated with childhood and horror, two of the most highly-charged taboos around. For many people anything that is off-limits becomes desirable. Or perhaps a clown fetish begins with imprinting. Maybe little Johnny got his first boner sitting on the lap of a clown, or Bozo's big feet felt good on little Janey's clit as she played airplane on his shoe" (Bruce 2002).

Whatever its origins, clown porn became a thing around the turn of the last century. *Clown Porn*, the film, was the brainchild of Ocean Beach, California, resident Chris Spoto. He formed a production company called Ramco in 2004 and released a video the following year. In a 2011 interview with the *San Diego City Beat* newspaper, Spoto discussed the unanticipated difficulties he faced as a pioneer in the then-unplowed field of clown pornography:

We learned the first day of shooting that the makeup, especially when they start getting hot and heavy, gets smeared all over everything. [Lead actress] Hollie Stevens was the one. She said, 'It's a clown thing; don't worry about it.' So, we just accepted it and went with it. By the end of most of these scenes, there's clown makeup everywhere and, actually, there's a lot of fetish people who really dig this stuff because of the mess that's made. Again, it's not what we were shooting for, but we touch upon a lot of fetishes accidentally. It comes from your typical clown-association things—like, we use cream pies. Well, that is an absolute niche fetish. There's—let's see, I forget what it's called—splatter? People who get off on cream pies. And then there are the balloon people. (Morlan 2011)

Spoto noted that he'd never really intended to break new ground: "It really wasn't so much about making porn as it was dealing with my irrational fear of clowns. I've had a lot of time to think about it and that's what it really boils down to. I don't really know *why* clowns but I know that once the decision was made, there it was" (ibid.).

The reviews for *Clown Porn* were mixed; one charitable reviewer opined:

Clown Porn reveals the fang-mouthed menace of movie clowns like Pennywise from *It* for the silly shams they are. These are *real* clowns and they are *really* having sex with women. There can be no doubt or room for comforting thoughts of movie magic. You see the rubber chicken being mashed against breast and the smudge of transferred makeup around razor-burned vulva. You hear the honking of horn and wet splat of whipped cream pie on the face of an unlucky victim. You will witness the terror of clowns ejaculating and being ejaculated upon, and once you have it is something you can't unwatch. Pray for a miracle. Pray for a stroke. It won't matter. The images will race through dead cells, leap like lightning across burned out neural pathways, and sear themselves into the backs of your eyes like the word PAUSE into the center of your old TV. A knitting needle in your eye will make you forget your own name, but it won't ever take away *Clown Porn*. (Parsons 2005)

Clown Porn spawned other adult films featuring clowns, including the Ass Clowns series from a company called Extreme Associates. One of the films, *Ass Clowns 3*, has the dubious distinction of being one of five movies that served as the basis for a 2005 federal obscenity case, *United States v. Extreme Associates*. According to one review of that film, actress Bree Brooks appears on camera having sex with the character John Merrick, better known as the Elephant Man: "Not only does she have to service this mutant's long rod, she has to do so while being slapped and chafed and screamed at by an evil clown in a coat-and-tie and baseball cap" (Ross 2002). I'll spare the gentle reader further elaboration.[1]

While the erotic merits of clown porn may be subject to individual taste, some came to view it as a public menace and a group called Stop Clown Porn Now emerged. It's not clear whether the group's protest was a lighthearted, satirical prank (see chapter 10) or a serious cause for the social-justice crowd looking for a new subject to fuel their outrage (the two are often indistinguishable). Sarah Woodstock, a writer for Urbanette.com, conducted a (possibly fictional) interview with "Infozo," a representative of the group, who described it as a loosely organized and affiliated grassroots campaign out to put an end to the travesty that is Clown Pornography. Our members organize protests against clown pornographers and in support of legitimate, non-porno clowns; we also try to provide local support for clowns in peril and persons afflicted with the clown paraphilia, sometimes called 'coulrophilia.' . . . Yes, we are serious. Clown pornography is a serious problem. The central problem with clown pornography is its too-often-conscious attempt to exploit the power that the clown archetype has in relation to each of our psyches. We graciously admit that, historically, the clown has been intimately associated with sexual antics, but the Ancient Greeks who placed huge phalloi on their comic actors are long dead, and so is the unholy common-law marriage of the clown and sexual abandon. To reintroduce sex to that archetype is to tinker with the fundamental structures of our collective psychology.

Infozo noted that "there are at least twenty professionally made adult videos that are available in the United States that depict clowns in sexually inappropriate scenarios. There are at least three *Penthouse* pictorials in which the models are made up like clowns, three *Playboy* pictorials, and a handful of picture spreads in less reputable glossy-print girlie mags. There are hundreds of pornographic Web sites featuring either real clowns, models dressed as clowns, or non-clown pornographic models who have been digitally remastered of the clown in a sick effort to snake a buck from the fetishist population" (Woodstock 2008). The website StopClownPornNow.org is no longer active (as of late 2015), though T-shirts are sold featuring the website URL below an image of a clown with a ball gag in his mouth, and below the classic social-justice slogan "Will you speak out for those who cannot speak for themselves?"

The clowning profession has quite understandably and sensibly ignored the clown-porn subgenre (any protests by clown organizations would only provide publicity for the films), and interest in the films seems to have faded in recent years. Though most clown porn is visual, clown-themed erotica does exist. The realm of written clown porn is not very wide but it does plough deep; one resource for what are delicately described as "Clown Sex Stories" appears on the website cuntcircus.com.

As of late 2015 there were four stories there, with such titles as "After Party" and "My First Time with a Clown." Here's a sample:

> It was my nephew's seventh birthday. I knew a clown was going to be at the party, they had found one in the phone book and hired her sight-unseen. I expected some overweight middle-aged woman to show up. Oh, how wrong I was! Turned out the clown for the day was a petite 21-year-old working weekends to pay her way through college. 'Bubbles' was dressed in full clown regalia, with a bright orange wig, white face makeup, and even a rubber nose. Instead of baggy pants, though, she had on a short poofy skirt and rainbow-colored tights. I couldn't keep my eyes off of this little bundle of energy. Her act was practically acrobatic, with her contortions revealing her firm legs and an ass that redefined 'bubble butt.' She caught me staring at her a few times and met my glance with a mischievous smile, sending shivers up my spine and producing a circus-scale tent in my pants.

Those seeking more literary clown porn may enjoy the 2007 book *Clown Girl: A Novel*, by Monica Drake, with an introduction by *Fight Club* author Chuck Palahniuk, about a part-time clown named Sniffles who becomes involved with clown sex work.

Ouchy the S&M Clown

Clown-themed porn and stories are fine, but for those who want a more real-world take on sexy clowns, it's hard to beat Ouchy the S&M Clown (see plate 17). If Ouchy was on a carnival midway and had his own talker—not barker, real carnies never use the word *barker*—out front to turn the tip, we can imagine the rehearsed spiel: "Come one, come all! He puts the 'ow!' in clown, and the 'slap' in slapstick. . . . He's Ouchy the S&M Clown! He's here, he's live, and he's inside! Get your kinks on Route 66!"

Ouchy is a bisexual white-faced California clown with a fondness for black leather. I spoke to Ouchy from two states away via the safety of a telephone, and even then there was a certain menace in his voice that hinted of familiarity with rough trade. In case there's any confusion about what exactly he does, Ouchy set the record straight right up front: "I am a dom [domination] clown, a pervert clown. . . . And I don't do kid's parties" (Ouchy the Clown 2008).

Never having spoken with a pervert clown—or at least not one freely introduced as such—I asked what it took to make that a profession. It turned out that the requirements for being a pervert clown are specific but minimal. "Well, being a pervert certainly helps, and not being shy. In this line of work, it helps if you like to hurt people. . . . Having a sadistic streak definitely helps."

Ouchy has been dispensing domination in San Francisco's Bay Area since 2001. "I'd been going to BDSM [bondage and domination / sadism and masochism] parties and learning about the whole scene. One of the things I realized pretty quickly is that the BDSM community takes themselves *very* seriously." (As he paused I could almost hear the sound of eyes rolling under greasepaint.) "Which was fine, but it wasn't really my thing. I wondered what would happen if I put a clown face on. I got such a crazy reaction, I knew I struck a nerve—and God knows I like to strike nerves."

And what does one get with his services, I asked?

"Oh, you know . . ." he began vaguely.

I actually *didn't* know, and frankly I was afraid that any wild guesses I might offer would either come off as sounding naive and prudish ("You show up at the door in drag with penis-shaped balloons?") or unreasonably perverted ("You pop out of a tiny clown car in a tutu and then masturbate onto a baby rhino's back while lip-synching to 'Relax' by Frankie Goes to Hollywood?"). I really had no frame of reference and briefly stammered, trying to fill in the blanks. Though I was feeling a bit uncomfortable, Ouchy wasn't getting paid for it and so he spoke up to relieve my pain: "I beat people. I do piercings, shave people with a straight razor, tell bad jokes, and generally be obnoxious. Most often I'm hired for bachelor or bachelorette parties, typically to abuse the guest of honor. I take out my double-sided, polka-dot St. Andrews cross and strap the person up to that."

And then? "And then I abuse them for as long as they can take it," he finishes. Ouchy's website gives a taste of what he offers: "As your clown dominant, I am your excruciating source for: Bondage and discipline; hot wax; straight razor shaving; boundary pushing; and making you laugh while I hurt you. I have been a practicing clown dom for over three years and am respectful of all limits. Trust me, I'm a clown" (Ouchy the Clown 2014).

On his website Ouchy also offers a small selection of porn reviews, mostly vintage but a few newer ones including *Johnny Toxic's Clown Fuckers*, described as "an XXX clown rated sex documentary about Johnny Toxic's cousin, Putzo The Clown. This is the 'true' story of his disgusting, nasty perverted life as a homeless Hollywood clown walking the streets and fucking slutty street trash ho's wherever and whenever he can! Stuffing them with Putzo choad and frosting them with funny goo! Join Putzo and his pals as they honk, bonk and toot the nastiest clown c*nts in Hollywood."

I asked Ouchy the S&M Clown about some of his most memorable gigs. "I had a quadriplegic ask me to beat him; that was interesting. . . . I was hired for an engaged couple at their party to put both of them on the cross and beat them simultaneously. It was arranged by a friend of theirs, who didn't tell them what was going on. They were surprised!"

He is of course aware of the evil-clown motif, and he plays with the archetype. "I don't see clowns as inherently bad," Ouchy says, "but they are inherently mysterious. I'm not afraid of clowns in the least, in fact, I find them quite fun. But some friends of mine have had weird experiences with clowns when they were younger that affected them. A lot of times the clown got in their face and scared the bejeesus out of them. I had one friend who was actually molested by a clown as a young kid."

Asked if he gets hate mail from Shriners who are angry at him for besmirching the good clown name, Ouchy says with an audible shrug, "I don't get any hate mail. I'm not exactly encroaching on balloon animal territory." The number of people requesting the services of a pervert clown has declined in recent years, and although Ouchy doesn't abuse as many people as he used to, he is still active and available for gigs all across the country. He can be found on Twitter and at www.ouchytheclown.com.

Crotchy the Masturbating Clown

No discussion of freaky clowns would be complete without the case of the clown who forced the Nebraska Supreme Court to watch him masturbate. Mat Honan, the former senior editor at the now-defunct webzine

GettingIt.com, begins the story: "In 1995, school bus driver/washer-cum-actor-cum-masturbating clown Scott Harrold . . . debuted a little show called *Cosmic Comedy* on Lincoln, Nebraska cable access television. The series featured Harrold, a.k.a. Crotchy the Clown, reviewing adult films—complete with clips—while dressed in clown garb. The local citizenry was dutifully appalled, but nothing could be done, as the show didn't meet the legal definition of obscenity."

The zero-budget *Cosmic Comedy* show, which aired around midnight, made *Wayne's World* look like *Avatar*. Most of the episodes dutifully carried a warning that the content was not suitable for kids—a point surely made clear when the host clown opined about which mid-1990s porn suited his "needs." The public access show and its handful of viewers continued unmolested until September 24, 1995, when Crotchy juggled one ball too many and crossed a line, slapping the clown on camera.

The video "featured Harrold as Cozblah, another of his clown characters, rambling incoherently and grunting into the camera for almost 15 minutes. Then the tape abruptly cut to a shot of Harrold dressed as Crotchy, or—to be exact—in Crotchy makeup but otherwise naked, reclining in a chair" before masturbating (Honan 1999). The court reviewed several of Harrold's videotapes (see plate 18) and dryly noted that

> approximately the last 1.5 to 2 minutes of Harrold's videotape is Harrold masturbating, while attired only in a clown face. In this part of the videotape, Harrold is shown alone, in a reclining position. He appears to be nude, except for a pair of shiny sunglasses which cover his eyes, and his face is painted as a clown with a dark beard and white lips. The camera capturing these images was apparently positioned between Harrold's legs, so that the principal image framed by the camera is Harrold's hands stroking his erect penis, although his chest and face are visible. After 1½ to 2 minutes, Harrold simply stops masturbating, and it appears from exhibit 2 that he does not ejaculate. Very little sound accompanies the images of Harrold masturbating. Toward the end of this scene, Harrold makes several largely unintelligible comments, except that one can hear the phrases "left wing" and "for the ladies." (*State of Nebraska v. Scott A. Harrold* 1998)

Crotchy later explained that he had conducted the "performance" at the request of one of his female viewers who wished to see more male nudity on the show.

The local public access company, CableVision, called the police, who cited Harrold for distributing pornography. Harrold was convicted, fined $1,000, and (not surprisingly) fired from his public school job. Harrold, citing his First Amendment rights, appealed his conviction and won on appeal in October 1998. The court decided that the masturbating clown's act—though offensive, bizarre, and "a Bozo no-no," did not meet the legal definition of obscenity and therefore was not pornographic. As Honan notes, the District Attorney's office was not about to let Crotchy's crime go unpunished: "Prosecutors took the case to the Nebraska Supreme Court, which would rule once and for all whether clown masturbation was a crime." At trial

> Harrold testified that he produced, directed, and often acted in the "Cosmic Comedy" episodes which he gave to CableVision for broadcast. Harrold explained that he designed the series to be an "experimental showcase," with a theme spoofing cheap science fiction films from the 1950s. Harrold stated that he had taken a course in "clowndom" at a local community college and that he had developed a cadre of a dozen or more clown characters who intermittently appeared on "Cosmic Comedy." These characters included clowns named "Cozblah" and "Crotchy," who appear in the episode at issue, and "Crappy," an older clown whom Harrold described as Crotchy's father. (*State of Nebraska v. Scott A. Harrold* 1998)

The basis for Harrold's conviction rested on the legal definition of obscenity, which depended on whether it appealed to a "prurient interest in sex," that is, it was intended to turn someone on. The Supreme Court concluded that Crotchy's masturbation performance, though seltzer-free, was intended to appeal to at least one person: the female viewer who wrote in asking for more male nudity (though, it should be noted, it's not clear that she was hoping to see a naked clown rubbing one out while generously declaring, "This one's for the ladies"). Therefore Harrold was indeed guilty of distributing obscenity and hence the pornography conviction was reinstated.

It's not clear whatever became of Crotchy the Masturbating Clown; he seems to have given up the fight and moved on. However in 2013 an online poster using the name Cozblah (the name that Harrold appeared under in the videotape that led to his conviction) came to Crotchy's defense nearly twenty years after the episode aired. In a rambling, angry post Cozblah wrote in part (and verbatim, *sic* throughout):

> While crotchy the clown and COSMIC comedy copyrighted 1994 is NOW world wide copys of copys of copys with ripped off copyrighted arts, the paperback hacks will rewrite even court room transcipts into nothingness for profits also. SPICE time warner cable fully adult porno ran at the sametime as cosmic comedy but yet no charges were ever given the network 24 hour full time adult xxx channel. . . . FREEDOM of the arts is NOT for the non monoplyous but only for the profit corperation which oans and controls the airwaves same as predicted by the CIA in the eraly 1970's. . . . SHUT up about crotchy the clown cozblah and COSMIC COMEDY paperback cons you know nothing about those subjects or freedom of the arts and those adult subjects that are not allowed by our courts. Crotchy the clown never engaged in sex on screen was enever with anyone never engaged in any banned subject matter but was yet banned and copied while adult muti billion dollar chanel ran 247 365 and those xxx networks are still up and running while even after nearly 20 years the hacks for the network SS [presumably a reference to Hitler's SS troops] still shovel dirt on crotchy's grave for aliving just as the CIA predicted in 1976. (Cozblah 2013)

If those are indeed the final ramblings of Crotchy the Masturbating Clown, at least he's typing on the computer and keeping it in his pants.

CHAPTER 9

Creepy, Criminal, and Killer Clowns

There are countless real-world creepy, criminal, and killer clowns that have roamed the planet at one time or another. Here are some of the most notorious.

Stalking Clowns

Over the years a handful of clowns have appeared in cities around the world with the apparent intent to frighten and unnerve the public. When a clown trods on private property unbidden, that's a trespassing crime that may cause the authorities to get involved and possibly arrest the clown. Clowns appearing in public are another matter; there is no law against anyone dressed in a costume, jesterish or otherwise, walking down the street or visiting a public park. Several of the most famous stalking clowns have appeared in Northampton, England; New York; California; and France.

THE NORTHAMPTON CLOWN

A mysterious and sinister clown prowled the streets of Northampton, United Kingdom, in 2013, causing both curiosity and concern. Nocturnal sightings of the face-painted fiend—widely dubbed the Northampton

Clown—began in early October. The clown did not harass, attack, nor threaten anyone; he—or possibly it—merely wandered the streets creeping people out (and sometimes posing for photos). Typically he was unnervingly silent but on occasion he would menacingly blurt out, "Beep beep!" quoting Stephen King's killer clown Pennywise.

A Facebook page was set up on Friday the Thirteenth, appropriately enough, called "Spot Northampton's Clown," featuring photos of the clown at different locations throughout the city. Someone claiming to be the clown posted photos, updates, and notes saying he was harmless and just having a bit of fun. At first it all seemed like a viral prank, publicity stunt, or theatrical melodrama. In fact, a second man—dressed in his own blue, muscle-padded superhero costume and glasses calling himself "Boris the Clown Catcher"—soon appeared on Northampton streets on a mission to capture the creepy clown. Some suggested that Boris himself was the Northampton Clown, adopting the role of both hero and villain in an episode of performance art or social-media prank.

The Northampton Clown, on the other hand, was real enough. Though the clown undoubtedly made some people genuinely uneasy, most of the discussion and controversy was conducted with tongues firmly planted in cheeks. The fact that the clown happily posed for curious bystanders suggested an element of hoaxing or mischief; after all, if anyone thought the clown was a serious threat they could follow him to his lair or call police. It's also important to note that England has, by some estimates, nearly 2 million surveillance cameras in operation. Public streets are routinely monitored and recorded, and it would be a simple matter for police to review footage to locate a doorway or vehicle where the clown emerged. That is, of course, assuming that they believed there was any public threat; as noted, walking around dressed as a clown at night is not illegal.

The Northampton Clown was eventually unmasked without a drop of blood spilled. Connor Simpson, writing for TheWire.com, noted on October 16, 2013, that

> the identity of the Northampton clown, who terrorized a city for an entire month, was finally revealed. The Northampton clown's identity was Europe's greatest mystery ever since the creepy costumed

comedian began terrorizing the small British town from which he takes his name last month. Residents started tracking his whereabouts with a hashtag and a Facebook group as he continued popping up around town, scaring kids and avoiding vigilantes dedicated to catching and unmasking the clown's dastardly plot. His identity remained a mystery until last weekend, when the *Daily Mirror* confirmed Alex Powell, a 22-year-old local filmmaker, and his two accomplices, Elliot Simpson, a fellow local filmmaker, and Luke Ubanski, who ran the clown's Facebook page. (Simpson 2013)

A reporter for the *Northants Herald and Post*, Steve Scoles (2013), was the first to suggest that Powell was the mysterious clown, noting that "sensational footage has emerged which appears to show the notorious Northampton clown starring in a short movie on YouTube. The film by Alex Powell is called *The Local Clown: A Short Mocumentary* and features a clown called Richard dressed identically to the Northampton clown in a blue suit and yellow shirt. It was posted four months ago" (Scoles 2013). Powell had repeatedly denied being the clown in Facebook posts and in interviews, but finally admitted it when reporters arrived at his doorstep with photographs implicating him.

It was all a bit of harmless fun for Powell and his friends—though it did spawn hate mail and death threats along with complimentary comments from delighted mystery lovers. "On Facebook I've had over a thousand death threats," he told the *Daily Mirror*. "'It was just a bit of fun at first and a lot of people seem to enjoy it but it gets a bit hard sometimes with the death threats.' Powell . . . claimed a man threatened to knife him. . . . 'I swear he had a knife and told me he would stab me if there were not so many people around. . . . I had a call last night from someone who knew my name and asked if I was the clown and said if they saw me they would run me over'" (Simpson 2013).

Not content to merely freak out Northampton residents, the clown (or, presumably Powell) later turned to writing his memoirs. Swapping his balloons for a keyboard, in 2013 the Northampton Clown wrote the book *21 Insights into the Happy Life of the Northampton Clown*. He explains his goals upfront: "As a means of helping all of you human mortals understand my perspective, I've decided to write this book. I thought that perhaps you might not only learn to see things from my 'happy' perspective, but you could also learn a bit more about my life as a clown. I want you to get to know me a bit better. Maybe then you'll appreciate me the next time you spot me in Northampton. That is of course, if you're not too completely terrified. In this book, I am going to reveal some thing that you have been wanting to know about me. I am going to give you 21 insights into my, not psychotic but 'happy' life." The book is a breezy ninety-two-page read touching on a variety of subjects ranging from his rise to fame, his visit to Stonehenge, and the "Zombie Clown Apocalypse." The Northampton Clown's biggest legacy, however, is probably reflected in the number of copycats he inspired.

THE STATEN ISLAND CLOWN

Less than six months after the Northampton Clown scare faded, a mysterious and apparently malevolent clown began lurking on the roads of the New York City borough of Staten Island. Taking a cue from the social-media savvy that helped the Northampton Clown become an international figure of mystery, the clown began appearing on Facebook and Instagram, where four people first posted snapshots of the clown in early March 2014. In one widely circulated photo the balloon-bearing, bald-capped buffoon is standing near a road detour sign near the Richmond Valley train station waving at passersby; in another image he (or perhaps she, it's not clear) is skulking behind a tree. The "SI Clown," as it was soon dubbed, bore a striking resemblance to Stephen King's Pennywise, leading to a cheeky March 28 tweet from the horror king: "Pennywise spotted on Staten Island. Do I get royalties? #SIClown" (see plate 19).

The *New York Post* looked into it and deemed the sightings a publicity stunt. Part of the story of the SI Clown unraveled when reporters realized that the four people who originally posted photos and videos of the clown on social media were not random Staten Island citizens who happened to stumble across the clown as he wandered the streets, as might be expected. Instead, the four not only knew each other but, it turned out, had professional affiliations with the same Staten Island–based production company called Fuzz on the Lens—one that produces horror films.

It was a clever, if short-lived, publicity stunt. Given the public's curiosity about scary clowns, and the near certainty that images of anonymous, creepy clowns would go viral on social media, it worked out well. The film company was coy at first about whether it was behind the SI Clown scare, neither confirming nor denying it and instead tweeting a cryptic message: "Kinda insulted by all these #SIClown accusations . . . we're not just a 'horror film company.' (We're funny too . . . I swear)."

But soon Fuzz on the Lens copped to causing the clown concern with a follow-up tweet: "Well . . . you got us. We'll admit it. Retweet if you like the #SIClown and favorite if you'd rather not see him anymore," along with a photo of the clown in a police-style lineup with five other men holding signs reading, "Fuzz on the Lens Productions." With that confirmation of what many suspected—and like the Northampton Clown before him—the mystery behind the Staten Island Clown finally crumbled. The *New York Daily News* ran a story announcing that

the creepy bozo who used the cover of night to frighten unsuspecting Staten Island residents has finally been unmasked. As suspected, the clown is the brainchild of Fuzz on the Lens Productions. The Staten Island film company confessed on Twitter Friday. Filmmaker Michael Leavy denied that the ploy was a publicity stunt for a movie. "We treated this as a film within itself . . . we treated him as a character and the world was our production," Leavy said. . . . the film production company later released a short on YouTube detailing how they captured the clown and brought him to justice. (Kuruvilla 2014)

CREEPY CALIFORNIA CLOWNS

Later that year and shortly before Halloween 2014, residents in the California towns of Bakersfield and Wasco were plagued by stalking, scary clowns. The clowns began appearing in late September, often at night. Sometimes people saw the clowns, staring at them silently from a street corner or darkened parking lot. Often, however—in apparent imitation of the Northampton Clown and the Staten Island Clown the year before—the clowns were photographed in front of various city landmarks, the images then shared on social media. While most of the clowns held nothing more sinister than a creepy scowl and a handful of balloons, some were seen and photographed wielding large weapons such as machetes or baseball bats. Some people were scared, some were amused, and some called police though there were no reports of anyone threatened or hurt. ABC News reported that "police say the clowns weren't generally engaging in criminal activity. There was only one arrest, of a juvenile, last week in Bakersfield. He was allegedly chasing other juveniles while dressed as a clown, and told police he was doing it because of a hoax he had seen online"—essentially a copycat of a copycat of a copycat (Murray 2014).

So who or what was behind the mask? A news report on the local site KernGoldenEmpire.com stated that the Wasco clown photos were part of a photography project: "An interview with the Wasco clown, who requested to remain anonymous, revealed that the social media postings are part of a year-long photography project conducted by his wife. The couple will be posting the pictures from their photoshoot every day this month.... The photographed clown and his wife said they did not expect to start a trend, and did not mean to cause any harm" (KernGolden Empire.com 2014). The clown sightings soon faded away—in the United States, anyway.

THE 2014 FRENCH CLOWN PANIC

Around the time of the California clown scare, a cluster of reports swept across France. According to one report, "the phenomenon of dressing up as an evil clown and terrifying passers-by—a trend which has also been seen in the United States and Britain—cropped up in the north of France in early October. In the town of Bethune, a 19-year-old received a six-month suspended jail term last week for threatening passers-by while dressed as a clown. These 'clowns' have been 'mostly spotted outside schools, but also on public roads, in bushes, in a square. Their targets are often young children or teenagers, but also adults,' a police source in northern France told AFP" (AFP 2014). Anticlown gangs of vigilantes were soon organized, vowing to exact brutal revenge on any clowns who stepped out of line. According to Belgian folklorist Aurore Van De Winkel, the European clown panic "began in France on the 10th of October with a disguised teenager chasing his terrified neighbor with a plastic knife in downtown Périgueux (in the middle of France), simply as a practical joke" (Van De Winkel 2015).

Social media quickly spread rumors that bands of clowns armed with knives, machetes, and chainsaws had been attacking people across the country; some warned that public gatherings would be targeted by groups of hundreds of evil clowns. Despite the fact that no arrests had been made—and apparently no one had actually been injured or killed by the clowns—the rumors spread across Europe to Italy and elsewhere a week before Halloween.

While the first clown reports and pranks were clearly inspired by news-media reports from the United States (and the Wasco clown in particular) and online pranks and videos, malicious people began to use the clown-scare rumors as a cover to commit crimes. Some of these acts were likely copycats inspired by a series of hidden-camera videos created and shared online by DM Pranks, which depicted unwitting people in public places (such as a parking garage and a gas station) being confronted with a menacing, armed clown. In some of the videos the clown seems to be smashing a victim's head in with a huge mallet, complete with gory special effects.

Not merely copycats but criminals, the handful of "clowns" acted out—and adapted—what they had seen in the media (this is what in folklore is called ostension). For example,

On October 24, a young man disguised as a clown smashed a car in the Hérault, France. The following day, a pedestrian was attacked with an iron bar at Montpellier by a young man in clown make-up. This attacker was given a twelve month sentence, four of them incarcerated. On October 28 in Nivelles, Belgium, an eighteen year old man was severely beaten by two persons disguised in clown outfits for seemingly no reason at all. Two days later, in Luxembourg, a young man was reported to be a victim of a violent burglary committed by three or four men with clown masks. Attacked with a knife, he ended up in the hospital with eighteen stitches. On November 5, a ninety-year-old woman was attacked by two hostile clowns in Paris while she was withdrawing money from an ATM. They stole 300 euros from her account. (Van De Winkel 2015)

While the details in some of these reports remain unproven—it's possible that a few were made up or exaggerated for attention or sensationalized by news media—it's clear that at least a few real crimes were committed under the greasepainted guise of clowns. The clown panic faded away not long after that, leaving Europeans in its wake puzzled by what happened. (For a comprehensive analysis of the Halloween 2014 European clown attacks and copycats, see Van De Winkel 2015.)

According to a Halloween 2014 article in the *Atlantic*, "the situation in France has led one French town to ban clown costumes altogether, not just for Halloween but for the entire month of November. And though many of France's evil clowns have been teenaged pranksters, their weapons—including baseball bats, knives, axes, pistols, and chainsaws—are often quite real. On Monday, a student in Besançon, in eastern France, cut his hand while apparently raising it to defend himself from an axe-wielding clown impostor. Other incidents have involved direct assault: in Montpellier, a clown and two accomplices beat a 35-year-old man with an iron bar in an attempted robbery" (Goldhammer 2014).

The French clown scare came around the time of the California pranks, strongly suggesting that copycats were involved, and indeed

the French police have blamed social media, as well as foreign influence. After a group of chainsaw-wielding clowns appeared in front of a primary school in northern France, the police suggested on Twitter that the clown gangs were taking their cues from the 1974 U.S. film *The Texas Chainsaw Massacre*. Some of France's major newspapers, too, have cited trends in Italy and America as possible sources of evil-clown inspiration. Le Monde speculated about the influence of DM Pranks, a YouTube account run by the Italian duo Diego Dolciami and Matteo Moroni, whose trilogy of "Killer Clown Scare Prank" videos has earned tens of millions of views. The videos show Dolciami in a clown costume smashing dummy corpses with a mallet while Moroni films the reactions of terrified passersby. (Goldhammer 2014)

The 2014 French clown scare, like the others, was short-lived. A few people were scared, a few were even injured, and a few had some good laughs.

The creepy clown reports surfaced again the following year when a clown in full regalia was spotted just outside Chicago's historic Rosehill Cemetery in July 2015. The clown waited to be spotted in the headlights of a passing car before scaling a seven-foot fence and running into the cemetery. No vandalism was reported, and the clown was never caught (Radford 2015a). Given how easy it is to create a copycat clown scare, it's likely that the world hasn't seen the last of these creepy stalking clowns.

DEVILLE THE EVIL BIRTHDAY CLOWN

In at least one case, it was reported that parents could hire a scary clown to stalk their children, as a sort of demented prank. In 2010 parents heard about an unusual service offered by a seemingly creepy—if not downright evil—Swiss clown. According to an article in the *Huffington Post*, "Just in case your children don't have anything to talk about in therapy, here's something you might want to consider: Dominic Deville rents himself out as an 'evil birthday clown' who leaves scary notes for your children, warning them that they're being watched and that they'll soon be attacked. At the end of a terrifying week, your child will indeed be attacked. Deville, wearing a freaky clown mask, will smash a cake into your child's face" (Campbell 2012).

It certainly sounds like a terrifying birthday prank, and it's probably a birthday gift that any divorced parents who don't want to lose custody of their kids might want to avoid. Despite several sensational and erroneous reports in the news media, the truth is that Deville never had a full-time job scaring or stalking children on their birthdays. In a 2012 interview about a week after his unnerving child-stalking service made international news, Deville gave a brief interview to clear the air: "Yes, the Evil Birthday Clown did actually exist—however solely in my native Switzerland and only in the summer of 2010. For lack of time I decided to close down that service afterwards. I do want to take the chance and deliver some answers concerning the Evil Birthday Clown: 1) The clown could only be booked for adults, never for kids under the age of 18; 2) The service lasted for 5 days and cost 666 Swiss francs; 3) The Clown was in action 10 times in the summer of 2010. Roughly every second person got hit with a pie in the face" (Deville 2012). Of course the truth isn't as scary or evil as it first appeared. It was a fun lark, but Deville returned to work at his events-management company in Lucerne. So if some evil scary clown is stalking your child shortly before his or her birthday, seemingly lying in wait to throw a pie in his or her face, don't blame Deville, as he's retired.

Assaulting and Molesting Clowns

It should not surprise anyone that more than a few people have at one time or another dressed up as a clown and preyed on children. At first glance this might give parents second thoughts about hiring clowns, but it's important to remember that most of these bad clowns are not professional clowns at all. Anyone can put on clown makeup, dress as a clown, or even perform at a kids' party, just as anyone can perform as a magician or Santa Claus. These evil clowns are the rare and aberrant exceptions.

KLUTZO THE CLOWN AND OTHERS

One of the creepiest clowns may be Amon Paul Carlock, a Christian missionary from Illinois who visited orphanages in Mexico and the Philippines as Klutzo the Clown, allegedly molesting many of the orphans there. Carlock "worked at least four years as a Springfield police officer, hiring on in 1973. He also worked as an officer for the Grandview Police Department and as a trainer and counselor with the state Department of Corrections. He had a fondness for children, was a volunteer with Big Brothers/Big Sisters and performed as Klutzo the Clown in shows for kids. His problems with the law began in June 2007 when he returned home from a trip to the Philippines and was questioned by Immigration and Customs Enforcement agents at the San Francisco International Airport" (Rushton 2013).

According to details of the investigation appearing in a report by Michael Mitchell, a special agent with the Department of Homeland Security and made available on TheSmokingGun.com, upon arrival at the airport Carlock said that he had visited the Philippines

> to visit an orphanage named "House of Joy." Carlock said that he entertained orphans at House of Joy through his work as a clown.

Carlock said that he has visited House of Joy in the past for the same purpose, and that the arrangements were made through a friend he made on the Internet. Carlock further stated that he and his wife have been in the clown business for about ten years and that they entertain children at birthday parties and hospitals. . . . Because Carlock was returning from a country which is considered high risk for child sex tourism and child pornography, coupled with the fact that Carlock's stated purpose for his trip put him in direct contact with young children [investigators] deemed it appropriate to review the images on Carlock's digital media devices to ensure they did not contain any images of child pornography. . . . Images on Carlock's digital camera revealed numerous images of nude young males, appearing to be between the ages of five and ten years old, with exposed genitals. . . . A majority of the images of naked minor boys viewed on the laptop appeared to be pictures taken at the orphanage. Carlock later confirmed this to be true. (Mitchell 2007)

When asked why there were so many pictures of naked boys he replied, "That's how they live" (perhaps the answer seemed easier than convincing the police that he visited nudist orphanages) and stated that he had intended to show the photos to his church to demonstrate their dire need for donations since they obviously couldn't afford underwear. Furthermore, the police report noted, "According to Carlock's website, he is an ordained minister formerly with the Church of Nazarene and currently with the Missionary Church International. Carlock's website also states that he has been involved in pastoral ministry, Christian education, Christian camping, and evangelism since 1967." Three of the minors depicted in the photos were interviewed and "made sworn statements in which they stated that they woke up to Paul Carlock fondling and caressing their penis and that he walked out of the room when they awoke" (Mitchell 2007).

Based on this evidence Carlock was arrested, but he was never convicted. Accused individuals are presumed innocent until proven guilty in a court of law, and Carlock was never found guilty, nor even put on trial. Just over a month after he was booked in a county jail, he died while in custody. Though a cause of death was never conclusively determined, his widow filed a lawsuit over the death, claiming that the jail neglected his physical and mental health, resulting in kidney failure and his death.

Canadian clown Pierre Bessette was one of only a few sex offenders who performed as member of a professional clowning organization, in his native province of Quebec; he was arrested for sex offenses in 2003. The Canadian city of Brampton, citing cases of Bessette and others, considered an ordinance requiring clowns and other children's entertainers to be licensed, which would include a background check for criminal and sexual offenses. After protests by clowns and much discussion the city decided against the proposal. While licensing seemed like a good measure, it would have been difficult to implement for several reasons, including that many clowns and other children's entertainers perform in homes and on private property, making city notification difficult. Others objected to the added financial burden placed on clowns, and the extreme rarity of such crimes. As the *Toronto Star* reported, "City council turned around a resolution passed earlier in the year that would have created a licensing system for clowns and other children's entertainers. Instead, councillors reopened the previous decision and voted to go with a staff recommendation calling on the city to develop an awareness campaign and to send the resolution to municipal agencies and the province, asking them to work toward child protection in the field of children's entertainment" (Grewal 2013).

In May 2004 a circus clown named Spanky was arrested and charged with ten counts of third-degree sexual exploitation of a minor. "Thomas Riccio, known as Spanky the Clown in his job with Ringling Bros. & Barnum and Bailey Circus, was charged . . . with 10 counts of sexual exploitation of a minor after state and federal police agents found him in Fayetteville, N.C. . . . Riccio, 23, became a clown in November, police said. He was with the circus when state and federal agents seized his computer that included hundreds of pictures of child pornography, police said" (Schoettler 2004). Riccio was caught as part of an international child pornography investigation; police located him by tracing his credit card information from porn websites. The arrest was, of course, a huge embarrassment and public relations nightmare for the circus, though there is no suggestion or evidence that Riccio sexually assaulted anyone at work or while in costume as a clown. Though news of his arrest was widely disseminated, there seems to be no record of his trial or conviction, and it is likely that the charges against him were quietly dropped.

In Wisconsin Ronald Schroeder, a former professional clown who worked as Silly the Clown, was arrested in 2007, accused of sexually assaulting his (adult) girlfriend and photographing her nude while she slept. In his 2008 trial he was accused of thirty-two charges and found guilty on twenty-nine of them, two of them for assault and the remainder for the photographs he took (Associated Press 2008). Schroeder was released from prison in October 2013 after serving six years in prison for the sexual assault charges (Bee 2013). Other clowns arrested or convicted of crimes include Canadian Randy Miller (Honker the Clown), sentenced to two years for child porn in 2011 (Elliot 2010), and Johnny Goodman, who stole a bicycle at the 2005 Burning Man festival while dressed as a clown and was later identified through social media, beaten up, arrested, and banned from attending Burning Man for three years (WABC 2005).

Though these cases are unnerving, statistically children are in far greater danger of being physically or sexually abused by a parent or a caregiver than any stranger off the street—and certainly one dressed as a clown. The clowns described here are the rare exceptions, not the rule; in many cases the only reason that the perpetrator made the news is because there is some connection, however tenuous, to clowns. The clown connection is merely a sensational news hook widely embraced by journalists and the public. It's important to place the bad clowns described here in their true context as very rare exceptions to the good clowns.

Killer Clowns

Last but not least we have killer clowns: real-life bad clowns who killed people, or tried to.

JOHN WAYNE GACY

When people think of real-life killer clowns, the one name that invariably comes up is Gacy, as in serial killer John Wayne Gacy. Though hundreds of serial killers have stalked North America, Gacy is one of the few with global notoriety, in the same class as Ted Bundy, Charles Manson, Richard "The Night Stalker" Ramirez, David "Son of Sam" Berkowitz, and Jeffrey Dahmer. Other killers have exceeded his body count, but few have been more vicious, and none have been as closely associated with clowns.

John Gacy preyed on young men, street hustlers, and drug addicts from 1972 to 1978, killing most of them by stabbing and strangulation. As Colin Evans notes in his book *The Casebook of Forensic Detection*, "Gacy had cruised Chicago's Bughouse Square district, trolling for young males, enticing them into his black Oldsmobile with offers of marijuana. Those who succumbed to his savage sexual demands were released, bleeding and battered; those who didn't were chloroformed into insensibility, raped, and then killed. Gacy tapped into another source of victims by offering five-dollar-per-hour jobs with his contracting business" (Evans 1996, 134).

Gacy buried twenty-eight victims on his property, mostly under the crawl space of his home, with the decaying corpses emitting a foul odor he dismissed as a "sewer problem." When he ran out of space under his floor he began dumping his victims in a nearby river.

Gacy enjoyed playing a cat-and-mouse game with the police, even when he knew he was being followed. According to FBI profiler John Douglas, Gacy "took it as a joke, even inviting two of the detectives to dinner. Knowing the police would not want to pick him up on anything trivial, he toyed with them by openly defying traffic laws and smoking marijuana. The pressure continued to grow, though, and Gacy finally cracked. He invited police right into his house, where they smelled rotting flesh" (Douglas and Olshaker 1997, 105). In all Gacy was accused of killing thirty-three people, nine of whom were never identified. After a lengthy and sordid trial Gacy was found guilty, imprisoned, and eventually executed by lethal injection on May 11, 1994, in Joliet, Illinois.

In interviews after his arrest Gacy discussed his role as a clown.

"Two of the Keystone Cops that had been following me were eating at a restaurant," said Gacy, "and they were asking me why I did clowning with all the other things I was doing, that I wouldn't have time. I told them because it was fun and was relaxing from my business. Going to the hospitals, visiting kids and old folks, was rewarding as well; and the parades were the most fun, as you could run off into the crowd, kiss the women, squeeze their breasts with husbands and boyfriends watching, and run off with them laughing, thinking it was funny. When you're in make-up clowns can get away with murder and no one gets mad." (Quoted in Barker 1997, 93)

Gacy's sensational reputation as the "Killer Clown" is only loosely based in fact. He did not work as a professional clown—he was a building contractor by trade—but he did occasional volunteer stints as a clown at various times, including at children's parties (he claimed to have worked at hospitals, though this has never been confirmed). His occasional forays as a clown had nothing to do with his serial killing, nor did he kill anyone while in costume. Clowning was a hobby he'd only done a few dozen times in his life, but nonetheless it cemented his gruesome reputation as a killer clown. Profiles of Gacy never fail to mention the fact that he played a clown—often highlighting it in the headlines or on the covers of books, films, and magazines.

Gacy devoted much of his incarceration to artwork, notes culture critic Mark Dery: "On death row, Gacy parlayed his meager artistic abilities into a lucrative mail-order business, selling crude, cartoony paintings to serial-killer fans: portraits of Elvis, Christ, Snow White and the Seven Dwarfs (!), and, most popularly, clowns: himself as Pogo; a skull in a ruffled collar and clown hat; an empty chair with a clown costume draped over it" (Dery 1999, 72). These are actively collected by serial-killer aficionados and murderabilia collectors (see plate 20).

For Halloween 2014 musician, actor, and director Rob Zombie created a haunted house featuring a room devoted to Gacy (along with other infamous serial killers such as Charles Manson, Ed Gein, and David Berkowitz) called Rob Zombie's Great American Nightmare. The haunted house stirred controversy because, as *Chicago Tribune* writer Luis Gomez noted, it is "located at the Odeum Expo Center in Villa Park—which is less than fifteen miles from where Gacy buried the majority of his thirty-plus murder victims in the 1970s—and includes an actor playing Gacy in clown attire inside a space meant to look like Gacy's living room" (Gomez 2014). Though Gacy's crimes occurred decades ago in Chicago, they still echo around the world, as they surely will for decades to come.

THE WEST PALM BEACH KILLER CLOWN

A Florida clown seems to have gotten away with murder in one of the strangest clown-related mysteries in history. It happened in West Palm Beach in the spring of 1990 when a woman named Marlene Warren heard a knock on her door at ten forty-five in the morning on May 26. She opened the door to find a white-faced clown wearing a bright red nose and an orange wig. The clown greeted Warren with a wordless nod and handed her a basket of red and white carnations, along with two silver balloons. As Warren looked down at the gifts she was receiving, the clown pulled out a gun and shot her once point-blank in the mouth with either a .38 or a .357.

According to Warren's son Joseph, who saw the shooting, the clown had brown eyes and wore army boots. The clown escaped in a white Chrysler LeBaron, which was later reported stolen and discovered abandoned. Warren died two days later in the hospital. Detectives at the Palm Beach County Sheriff's Office suspected her estranged husband Michael Warren of plotting the murder, along with a brown-eyed, brown-haired woman who worked repossessing cars for Mr. Warren's auto dealership. According to the *Gainesville Sun,*

> A woman matching the description of Sheila Keen, 27, bought a clown costume, makeup, an orange wig and a red clown nose two days before the murder, according to two West Palm Beach costume store clerks who tentatively identified Keen's photo from police files. Then, on the morning of the murder, a woman fitting Keen's description purchased two balloons and a floral arrangement at a Publix supermarket less than a mile from Keen's apartment, according to sheriff's documents. . . . The balloons and flowers match those left at the scene of the murder, according to the documents. Neighbors at Keen's apartment complex in suburban West Palm Beach said they frequently spotted Michael Warren, the dead woman's husband, at the complex, according to police reports. (Associated Press 1990)

Both Mr. Warren and Keen denied any involvement, either romantically with each other or in the death of Warren's wife. Keen claimed that she was out looking for cars to repossess at the time Mrs. Warren was shot. News of the killer clown shook the West Palm Beach community, and a news report dated a month after the shooting noted that "local adults and children are now apprehensive of businesses that employ [clowns]. 'Unfortunately, children are only hearing the negative side,' said Yvonne (Sunshine the Clown) Zarza, owner of Balloons Above the Palm Beaches. 'Normally, it's Don't go near a stranger. Now parents are saying, Don't go near clowns'" (*Globe and Mail* 1990). Warren stood trial in 1992 on 66 criminal counts of fraud, racketeering, and grand theft related to his business; on August 8 of that year he was convicted on over three dozen counts of fraud, grand theft, and petty theft (Folks 1992). No one has been charged in Marlene Warren's death, and her clown-clad murderer remains at large.

THE JOKER: LIFE IMITATES ART?

Because the DC Comics villain the Joker is by far the most famous bad clown in the world—having been depicted for decades in comic books, graphic novels, on television and in films by well-known actors, and so on—it's not surprising that the Clown Prince of Crime might have inspired real-life evil actions.

Conclusively establishing that a person committed a crime because of something they saw or read, be it a video game, movie, comic, or book, is difficult. People have long blamed fiction for causing real-life social problems, trying (with little success) to link violent video games to real-life violence, pornography to rape, and so on. Any piece of art with a high enough profile will reach hundreds of thousands, millions, or even billions of people. Out of those, a very few who already have a propensity for violence may act on their fantasies or pathological world views. J. D. Salinger's classic, *Catcher in the Rye*, for example, was read by tens of millions of people, including John Hinckley Jr., the would-be assassin of Ronald Reagan; Mark David Chapman, who shot and killed John Lennon; and other murderers. Salinger is no more responsible for the crimes committed by his readers than DC Comics is responsible for any crimes committed by fans of their characters. Nonetheless, there have been several high-profile crimes and murders blamed at least in part on the Joker as an inspiration.

James Holmes, the Joker?

Probably the best-known killer claimed to have been inspired by the Joker is James Holmes. On July 20, 2012, Holmes opened fire at a movie theater in Aurora, Colorado, killing twelve people and injuring dozens more. He showed up, apparently in costume, as many others did for a midnight premiere screening of the much-anticipated Batman film *The Dark Knight Rises*. The question immediately turned to motive: What would make a former university student commit such a horrific crime? The answer seemed obvious to many, and in the hours and weeks following the massacre the news media was abuzz with speculation that the dazed-looking Holmes had been inspired to kill by the Batman film where he executed his rampage. Many in the public, including journalists, pundits, and even some police officials assumed that there was a clear connection to either the Batman film or its characters. The 2014 documentary film *Killer Legends* links Holmes to the Joker, with writer/director Joshua Zeman stating that "Holmes's embodiment of the Joker . . . is no coincidence" (Zeman 2014). Media critics in particular used the shooting as an opportunity to criticize violent entertainment: Did fictional shootings, killing, and mayhem involving clowns lead to real-life tragedy?

The rampant speculation focused on several key pieces of evidence. It's easy to see why people would jump to the conclusion that the film and the massacre were related, but it's equally clear that the film itself did not inspire Holmes. The attack had been planned for months, starting long before the film had released; the audience he was part of, and that he fired on, was seeing the first screening of the film. Therefore *The Dark Knight Rises* could not have inspired his violent shooting, since Holmes himself had not even seen it.

The speculation then changed from suggesting that the film had inspired the killing to the idea that the film's villain, Bane, had been his inspiration. Even though Holmes could not have seen the film, trailers and publicity photos had been published showing Batman's nemesis, and he might have seen those and modeled Bane's murderous actions and garb.

Holmes was dressed in a bulletproof vest and a riot helmet at the time of his attack, along with a gas mask; in the film Bane also wears bulletproof armor and breathes through a mask (though not a gas mask). It could be seen as a case of a real-life fan dressing like a movie villain (this is nothing new, as legions of *Star Wars* and *Harry Potter* fans know), or it could merely be a case of dressing appropriately for the plan of attack: if a person is planning to be in a shootout and use a gas or smoke grenade, then a bulletproof vest and a gas mask are logical equipment for the purpose, and have nothing to do with Bane. Still, the connection was far from clear, and the news media finally settled on a different, and seemingly much more likely, Batman villain: the Joker.

Enter the Joker?

The speculation that James Holmes was inspired to kill in imitation of the famous fictional murderous clown rested on two pieces of evidence: the fact that Holmes had dyed his hair red or orange; and a claim made in news reports that just before he opened fire Holmes shouted, "I am the Joker!"

New York Police Commissioner Ray Kelly stated at a press conference that "it clearly looks like a deranged individual. He had his hair painted red, he said he was 'The Joker,' obviously the enemy of Batman." Such commentary launched a media frenzy; the *New York Daily News* stated that "the flame-haired freak accused of staging the *Dark Knight* movie massacre may have drawn inspiration from a twisted and even darker cinematic take on the classic Batman story. . . . The 24-year-old accused mass murderer dyed his hair and declared he was the Joker—Batman's arch-enemy—when he was arrested shortly after the massacre." An ABC News story added yet another element: "While there has been no indication as to the motives of James Holmes . . . new evidence suggests that he was inspired by the Batman series of comic books and/or movies. Law enforcement sources confirmed to ABC News that Holmes said 'I am the Joker' when apprehended by authorities. His hair was painted red [and] Holmes also booby-trapped his apartment, a favorite technique of the Joker" (Marikar 2012).

DC Comics was of course aghast that their most famous fictional villain might have inspired a real-life mass murderer and immediately issued press releases expressing their condolences and outrage. The film's opening was delayed, and Batman actor Christian Bale visited hospitalized shooting victims. It seemed to many that a real-life killer had indeed adopted an evil clown's persona to carry out his crimes.

However, as the weeks and months passed, what at first glance seemed like a clear-cut case of a mass murderer playing the Joker turned out to be far weaker than assumed. The claim that Holmes was inspired by the Joker would be much stronger if, for example, he had worn a Joker costume (which are relatively inexpensive and easily available), or if he had been in clown makeup. He did not wear the Joker's costume, or any makeup at all.

What about Holmes's dyed hair? For many people that was a clear an imitation of the Joker—but what the news media missed is that the Joker doesn't have red hair. Neither Joker in the films (played by Jack Nicholson and Heath Ledger) had red or orange hair: the Joker's hair is—and always has been—green. If Holmes was imitating the Joker, he seems to have done a very poor job of it, neglecting to adopt the character's makeup, hair color, costume, or any other characteristic of the iconic villain. In fact Holmes didn't use any part of the Joker's image in the attack.

But what about the numerous reports stating that Holmes explicitly claimed to be the Joker? As John Miller (2012) reported on the CBS show *Face the Nation*, that initial claim "turned out not to be true." In fact, Miller noted, "Every single witness that [the police] have spoken to, and that we [CBS News] have spoken to, has said that he did not say a word, he just opened fire. And in fact he was wearing a gas mask with a movie going on in the background so had he actually elected to say anything, no one would have heard him anyway."[1]

Claims about the Joker being an inspiration for Holmes's massacre gradually faded as it became clear that the connection was little more than a media-created myth. There was no mention at all of the Joker during Holmes's criminal trial in 2015; no Joker references surfaced despite extensive psychological examinations and investigations into the killer's past and motives. Nor was the Joker mentioned in notebook diaries kept by Holmes as he wrote down his plans to kill as many people as he could—not in imitation of any clown but because of what he described as his "lifelong hatred of mankind." Holmes pleaded not guilty by reason of insanity and was sentenced to life in prison in August 2015.

Thus—despite widespread speculation and reporting to the contrary— one of the worst mass murders in Colorado history turned out not to have been connected with evil clowns after all. Two years later, however, another series of murders did have a real connection to the Joker.

Jokers Wild in Las Vegas

On June 8, 2014, Jerad and Amanda Miller entered a pizza restaurant in Las Vegas, Nevada, and killed two police officers as they ate lunch. They then covered one officer's body with a Gadsden flag (bearing the familiar image of a coiled snake and the slogan "Don't Tread on Me") and pinned a note to the other officer's body that stated, "This is the beginning of the revolution." From there they moved to a nearby Walmart where Jerad Miller fired into the air, telling shoppers to get out and that they were witnessing a "revolution." Most people fled, though Jerad was confronted by a man carrying a handgun. He did not see Amanda Miller nearby; she shot and killed him. The pair then got more guns and ammunition from the Walmart displays. Police reinforcements arrived and following a quarter-hour firefight both Millers were wounded, Jerad critically. His wife shot herself in the head as police closed in and they both soon died (Bever 2014). The couple had prepared for an extended gunfight, well equipped with handguns, a pistol-grip shotgun, armor-piercing bullets, and food rations. When it was over five people were dead, including the Millers.

Though neither Miller had performed as a clown, they had both dressed as evil clowns. Specifically, Jerad Miller had often dressed up as the Joker—and his wife Amanda as Harley Quinn—not just once or twice on Halloween but on many occasions. Miller was clearly inspired by Heath Ledger's depiction of the Joker in the film *The Dark Knight*. In a widely circulated photograph prominently featured on many news sites (see figure 9.1) Miller is seen holding the Joker playing card (complete with the slightly bent upper right-hand corner) in exactly the same position—and in an identical purple gloved hand and with identical makeup—as Ledger in the film.

In one video uploaded to YouTube on October 15, 2012, and on the website Heavy.com on June 9, 2014, Miller appears in costume as the Joker, complete with green hair, purple jacket, and makeup. Standing in front of an American flag, he discusses a satirical campaign for the United States

FIGURE 9.1. A June 10, 2014, ABC News story about Jerad and Amanda Miller, anarchist killers who used the Joker's image. Screen capture from ABCNews.com.

presidency (Ornitz 2014): "My fellow Americans, I'm the Joker and I'm running for President because year after year I've watched you Americans—my fellow citizens—vote for tyranny. And it's always the lesser of two evils. . . . But we have a chance to make history, ladies and gentlemen. You can vote for the more evil."

He references a variety of conspiracy theories, including FEMA concentration camps, vaccines as agents of disease, the One World Government, and much more. He also states that Barack Obama plans at any moment to revoke Americans' right to own guns, which is ironic given that during Miller's standoff his wife shot and killed a man who confronted him with a legal handgun—presumably carried to prevent exactly the kind of killings that the Millers committed.

Though there seems no connection between the June 8 killings and the Joker, if there was ever a known killer emulating that evil clown, Jerad Miller was it. Yet when Miller made news, there was little or no speculation about a link between his crimes and the comic book character. Unlike James Holmes, few if any suggested that Miller was inspired to kill police because of an obsession with the Joker. Given the enthusiasm with which people blame fictional evils for real-world ones, it's curious that the Millers' massacre was not closely linked to the Joker character.

The most likely reason is that the Millers' antigovernment stance was clear from their words and actions. Indeed, "police said previously the Millers shared an ideology with militia and white supremacists that law enforcement officers were oppressors. The couple was kicked out of an encampment of supporters of Nevada rancher Cliven Bundy, who engaged in an armed standoff in April with federal Bureau of Land Management agents trying to round up Bundy cattle in a public land trespassing dispute" (Rittner 2014). Had the Millers' actions been less clearly motivated by antigovernment sentiment, it's likely that the Joker would have been implicated in the Las Vegas killings.

KOKO THE KILLER CLOWN

Koko the Killer Clown, a four-foot-tall dwarf, began working around 2000 at Coney Island's venerable Sideshow by the Seashore, along with various sideshow performers. Koko's selling points, according to the Coney Island Circus Sideshow website, include his "half prison uniform, half clown, wonderfully crude makeup, [and his] cage available for extra cost." Koko's murderous moniker is the result of his life of crime, though that didn't prevent his appearances in a handful of media outlets, ranging from the *RuPaul Show* to *Village Voice* to the *Maury Povich* show.

Cole Moreton, a reporter for the British newspaper the *Independent*, described his first meeting with Koko:

> Koko the Killer Clown was making balloon animals and telling us how he had come to this, performing on a gloomy stage by the seaside at the dog end of the season. There were only half a dozen people watching in the decrepit building on Surf Avenue, but none could take our eyes off the four-foot dwarf in the smudged greasepaint, or the warning on his Charles Manson T-shirt: "Don't F*** With Chuck." The little bundle of malice in a grey striped prison cap mumbled that he had been married once, until he caught "a gentleman" in bed with his wife. "I shot him in a particular part of his

anatomy," he said. "Not his head." One stubby arm made a dismissive gesture towards his groin. "It was the only place I could reach." (Moreton 2000)

ABC News reporter Buck Wolf offered his own short version of Koko's story of murderous revenge: he "was once a Ringling Bros. and Barnum & Bailey Circus clown. But when he caught his best friend in bed with his wife, he shot the man 69 times. Since he was a dwarf—and both men were standing—many of the bullets were lodged in the victim's crotch. Koko tells audiences at his Coney Island performances that he served six years of a 50-year sentence" (Wolf 2002).

Biographies of showmen and performers, of course, are about as pliable as a rubber chicken and as factually accurate as a sideshow banner. His story merits skepticism for several reasons, including that shooting a man sixty-nine times would require an awful lot of reloading and, likely, the tacit cooperation of the victim—unless of course Koko used a machine gun, in which case the gun's recoil might send the dwarf flying backward in spiraling backflips of rage. Plus, of course, a gun can be aimed so the bullets hit above eye level even if the shooter is crotch level.

Though Koko's murderous ways are likely merely sideshow lore, he is by many accounts notoriously surly. New York writer Charlie LeDuff described his Koko encounter in his book *Work and Other Sins: Life in New York City and Thereabouts.*

Koko the Killer Clown waddled with menace around the bar, a miniature baseball bat in his hand. His tiny fist clenched and unclenched its shaft, and his greasepaint smile turned into a frown. Another midget stood in the open-air entrance staring stupidly at Koko. "That guy gives little people a bad name," Koko announced to the bar, pointing a sausage-size finger at the interloper. "He has his nose in the air and besides he can't dance." The midget in the entrance began a mocking, little soft-shoe accompanied by a whistle blown in sharp, shrill bursts. A little girl looking down on the scene from her bar stool began to cry. . . . A rotund, developmentally disabled dwarf, Koko was the only performer I saw at Coney Island who might have earned a job as a freak in earlier days. . . . Lumbering onstage with his face slathered in black and white grease paint, Koko delivered a loud, atonal monologue as he struggled to make balloon animals. My response, shared by other audience members, was distinct discomfort. (LeDuff 2005, 166)

I'd hoped to interview the elusive dwarf to get the lowdown on the true nature of his maladjustment, but when I went in search of Koko, he'd vanished. A note on the Coney Island Circus Sideshow website as of January 2006 stated ominously, "Please note Koko has disappeared and we are no longer taking bookings for him." Three years later a 2009 topic on the Yelp New York website asked the public for information about the missing clown: "Where are you KoKo the killer clown?" a poster plaintively asked. Contacted in late 2014, Dick Zigun, his former manager at Sideshows by the Seashore, reported that he, like everyone else, had lost touch with Koko.

OTHER BAD CLOWNS

Francisco Rafael Arellano Felix, once head of the feared Arellano Felix drug clan, was killed in October 2013, shot dead by a clown during a party at his beachfront home in Cabo San Lucas, Mexico. His gang controlled the drug trade in Tijuana throughout the 1990s, though his power had waned under police prosecution and pressure from rival drug gangs. Felix and his organization partly inspired the 2000 Steven Soderbergh film *Traffic*. According to an ABC News report, "The gunman wore a clown costume, donning a wig and a red nose, the Associated Press reported. The killer's motive and choice of costume are under investigation" (Shaw 2013). At least three shots were fired; Felix was hit twice, once in the chest and once in the head. A short home video taken of the attack shows a clown wearing a bright-blue costume and a bright-pink curly wig walking behind a singer on stage. A few seconds later a series of gunshots are heard, then panicked screams. Though the clown is only seen very briefly, it appears to be the only known video taken of an assassin clown shortly before committing a murder.

The killer clown and one or more accomplices escaped and thus the motive remains unknown, though officials believe that Felix's murder was likely the work of rival drug gangs over unpaid debts and old grudges. Gang killings are routine in Mexico, and the slaying of an aging former leader would likely have made little news but for the disguise of his assassins, spawning sensational headlines like "Gunman Dressed as Clown Kills Former Mexican Drug Lord" (Shaw 2013).

Professional clown LeRoy Hullinger, better known as Buttons the Clown, was arrested in 1991 for hiring a hit man to kill his wife. He was in the midst of a divorce and was concerned that his wife would get custody of their children. Hullinger, who had worked as a professional clown in northwestern Ohio since 1983, offered an undercover police officer $400 and a used microwave oven as partial payment for his wife's murder. He was found guilty and sentenced to ten years in prison (Weiss 1991).[2]

Gangs of Clowns and Mara Salvatrucha

Clowns often appear in groups—popping out of tiny cars, getting into seltzer fights, and so on—so it should not surprise anyone that gangs of bad clowns have been reported. Juggalo gangs—fans of Insane Clown Posse—are covered in chapter 7. According to BBC News, "A gang of robbers dressed as clowns tied up a shopkeeper and pointed a shotgun at him before they were chased through Manchester city centre. . . . They handcuffed the trainee manager and threatened him with a sawn-off shotgun and a 10-inch knife before they fled with a small amount of money." The clowns jumped out of—and escaped in—a white Transit van that had been parked just outside the store (BBC News 2002).

Though the Juggalo gang threat may be exaggerated, there is a clown-related gang whose threat is both very real and internationally known. It is the Mara Salvatrucha, also known as MS-13, a criminal gang that originated in Los Angeles in the 1980s and has since spread to Canada, Mexico, and Central America. Consisting primarily of about seventy thousand members (mostly from El Salvador), the gang is notorious not only for their extreme brutality and cruelty, but also for their extensive, ornate tattoos, which often include clown faces and masks. As the book *Scary Clowns* notes, "Clowns are role models for members of the Mara Salvatrucha in El Salvador, because they represent 'the man who cries and laughs.' Gang members often have clowns tattooed on their bodies"

(Scary Clowns 2006, 118). Members of the Mara Salvatrucha have been found in Toronto, Canada, and the Canada Border Services Agency issued a handbook on gang tattoos to help its law enforcement officers identify members. It notes that "clown face/mask tattoos are common among gang members. The can have the following meanings: 'Laugh now, cry later'; 'Play now, pay later'; 'My happy life, my sad life'; 'Smile now, cry later'. This style of tattoo is typical among Latin and Asian gang members," including those in MS-13 (Canada Border Services Agency 2008).

In some cases African soldiers—or, more accurately, bands of young armed thugs who pass themselves off as soldiers—have donned colorful, clownlike costumes, including Day-Glo fright wigs, when going into battle. *Slate* writer Mark Scheffler notes that one of the most prominent examples was when the soldiers of Liberian rebel leader Charles Taylor (who later became president of that country) were "decked out in fright wigs and tattered wedding gowns" at the start of that country's 1989 civil war.

> During Taylor's rebel siege on Monrovia in the '90s, his band of dolled-up marauders . . . put on one of the most disturbing horror shows the planet has ever seen. Between 1989 and 1997, 150,000 Liberians were murdered, countless others were mutilated, and 25,000 women and girls were raped. . . . In an essay in *Liberian Studies Journal*, an administrator at Cuttington University College tells a story of Taylor's forces storming the rural campus during the initial stages of the war in "wedding [dresses], wigs, commencement gowns from high schools and several forms of 'voodoo' regalia. . . . [They] believed they could not be killed in battle." According to the soldiers themselves, cross-dressing is a military mind game, a tactic that instills fear in their rivals. It also makes the soldiers feel more invincible. This belief is founded on a regional superstition which holds that soldiers can "confuse the enemy's bullets" by assuming two identities simultaneously. (Scheffler 2003)

Belief in magic and witchcraft is strong in sub-Saharan Africa, and it is not uncommon for spells and talismans to be used in hopes of gaining personal or economic advantage. The unusual military garb not only provides the fighters with a sense of confidence and invincibility but also sends a strong message to their enemies, many of whom share those beliefs. A French or American soldier on a peacekeeping mission who encounters an armed man in crazy clownish fright wig may mock him, but an East African enemy will recognize the costume's significance—and may be intimidated or reluctant to engage him for fear that his protective magic is real.

In the weeks before Halloween 2014 clowns seemed to be in the news regularly. On October 24 police in Michigan's Blair Township received a 911 call from a man who complained that an armed man was "wearing camo pants and a clown mask and at one point was playing a trombone" in his garage. Police responded to find a drunken fifty-four-year-old man in a clown mask shooting a pellet gun at an aluminum can in the road. He was arrested for his own protection; the police report does not state if the man played the sad trombone as the officers arrived to handcuff him. The clown-faced drunk double-fisting a pellet gun and a trombone did not face jail time.

CHAPTER 10

Activist Clowns

The audience for most clowns is small. It may be a few people in a sideshow, a few dozen at a party, or a few hundred people under a circus tent. The act they perform is best suited for small groups and constrained geographically and socially. Some people, however, use clowns or clowning as part of a larger purpose: to effect social change.

Bring Me the Head of Ronald McDonald

For some the clown threat is not a personal one but instead a global and social one, with the clown dispensing not hissed, bourbon-scented threats or poisoned cotton candy but instead social injustice and economic violence. The original TV Ronald McDonald, played by Willard Scott, was unnerving enough but for some McDonald is not about clowning, or, really, even hamburgers; instead the clown symbolizes junk food and American capitalism. It's not the fault of the actors who have played him, nor the garish yellow-and-red costume; it's what he stands for, a globally recognizable mascot for a brand that, rightly or wrongly, symbolizes cheapness, excess, obesity, and imperialism.

Ronald McDonald, as a symbol freighted with social and political baggage, has been co-opted by many artists. In her anticorporate book *No Logo*, Naomi Klein explains why McDonald's is such an easy target:

FIGURE 10.1. Willard Scott as burger-loving, not-at-all-creepy early clown Ronald McDonald. Publicity still from the author's collection.

"McDonald's and Starbucks staff . . . frequently earn less than the employees of single-outlet restaurants and cafes, which explains why McDonald's is widely credited for pioneering the throwaway 'McJob' that the entire fast-food industry has since moved to emulate . . . international trade unionist Dan Gallin defined a McJob as 'a low skill, low pay, high stress, exhausting and unstable job'" (Klein 1999, 237). According to Klein, a 1986 protest by a group called London Greenpeace targeting McDonald's "was an early test case in using a single brand name to connect all the dots on the social agenda," including issues of rain forest depletion, Third World poverty, animal cruelty, unhealthy diets, waste production, poor labor conditions, and exploitative advertising (Klein 1999, 388). In the 2009 film *The Yes Men Fix the World*, the Yes Men prankster activists are seen producing a fake special edition of the *New York Times* that includes a variety of iconic figures in Ronald McDonald costumes and makeup, including Gandhi, Rosie the Riveter, Che Guevara, and Malcolm X, followed by the Golden Arches satirizing the slogan "I'm lovin' it" with "We're lovin' revolution."

With such a laundry list of grievances (whether real, exaggerated, or imagined) associated with McDonald's, it's no wonder that Ronald McDonald, as one of the world's most famous clowns, has come to symbolize a destructive influence.

Kalle Lasn, media critic and founder of *Adbusters* magazine, has targeted the hamburger chain for decades, complaining, for example, of "cultural homogenization" and "ongoing fast-food imperialism" (Lasn 1999, 150). McDonald's has been a regular target of *Adbusters*—especially through its most prominent corporate symbols, the signature golden arches and Ronald McDonald. In the November/December 2002 issue of *Adbusters*, for example, an article encouraged school students to "boycott World Children's Day visits from Ronald McDonald" and "Slap 'Bring the Clown Down' stickers around McDonald's." The magazine offered readers a stylized red, yellow, and white logo featuring a likeness of Ronald McDonald below the phrase "Bring the Clown Down" to be clipped out of the page, photocopied, and distributed as an act of consumer defiance and "culture jamming."

FIGURE 10.2. Anti–Ronald McDonald logo appearing in a 1999 campaign in *Adbusters* magazine to "Bring the Clown Down." Courtesy of Kalle Lasn and Adbusters.org, used by permission.

Ronald McDonald has been used in political posters as well, including Richard Sperry's "Machine Gun in the Clown's Hand," an antiwar print depicting George W. Bush and his archenemy Osama bin Laden both dressed as Ronald McDonald (see plate 21).

Bush holds an assault rifle as warplanes fly in formation above an inferno behind them. Bush's Mickey Mouse ears reference that president's

FIGURE 10.3. Ronald McHitler button created by Noah Lyon. Photographed at the New York Museum of Modern Art, 2014. Photograph and element arrangement by the author.

unsophisticated approach to foreign policy, and the pretzel hanging by a string around his neck references an incident in January 2002 when an encounter with a disagreeable pretzel left the leader of the free world bruised and unconscious. Another artist, Noah Lyon, added the stern look and distinctive mustache of Adolf Hitler to the mascot, creating a "Ronald McHitler" that appears on buttons sold at art museums.

Obama as the Joker

While Ronald McDonald has been a target for decades, one recent sociopolitical expression of the evil clown occurred in mid-2009. It all began rather quietly and inconspicuously: "On August 3, 2009, the *Los Angeles Times* reported that a mysterious poster had begun appearing on Los Angeles freeways and on-ramps. Sectioned into four discrete cells, the poster recalls an Andy Warhol print and features a photoshopped image of Barack Obama as Heath Ledger's Joker. His mouth a ghastly, blood-stained grimace, Obama's skin is white-washed and his eyes black-rimmed; the word 'socialism' cuts across his chest, suggesting that whatever this poster is trying to say, it isn't a compliment" (Phillips 2015, 97–98). It wasn't just any clown's face, nor just any bad clown's face: it was distinctively that of the murderous psychopathic clown the Joker.

This blend of art, apparent social activism (whatever its intent), politics, and pop culture proved irresistible and the story made national headlines. Though ostensibly an ambiguous piece of street art not unlike, perhaps, a Banksy or Shepard Fairey (who created the iconic Obama "Hope" image, which used an Associated Press photograph without attribution) the Obama-as-evil-clown image resonated with many people. A writer for the *Guardian* newspaper described the poster as "the single most chilling—and brilliant—piece of poisonous political propaganda I think I have ever seen" (Bradshaw 2009). Republicans gleefully shared the image, and "right-wing bloggers were quick to attribute the image to an organized, grassroots effort to contest Obama's allegedly socialist agenda." Democrats, meanwhile, took affront: "After months of racially charged attacks against the president, liberals couldn't help but see racism in the Obama/Joker image" (Phillips 2015, 103). The white face paint on a black man echoed blackface in a way that was hard to miss.

Who had blended the world's most famous president with the world's most famous evil clown? The true identity of the Obama-as-Joker artist was revealed on August 17, 2009, not as a political zealot at all but instead as a college senior in Illinois named Firas Alkhateeb. As a fun project to hone his Photoshop skills Alkhateeb had used an image of the cover of *Time* magazine featuring Obama and had tweaked it to add the Joker's features (many other famous people and even animals were similarly "Jokerized"). He then posted it—sans any socialist commentary—to his Flikr account where some unknown person later downloaded it and added the "Socialism" caption. It later resurfaced as street art. Alkhateeb evidently knew nothing about it and was as surprised as anyone when his image turned up on a Los Angeles street; in fact one news story explicitly noted that "Alkhateeb does not agree with the 'socialism' label that was attached to it" (Chow 2009). (For an in-depth analysis of this meme and how it was appropriated by the Internet community and spread by online trolls, see chapter 6 in Whitney Phillips's *This Is Why We Can't Have Nice Things*.)

The motivations for one or more people taking Alkhateeb's ostensibly innocuous art project, adding a "socialism" tag to it, and transforming it from an Internet meme into street art may never be known, and in a way it doesn't matter. The more interesting issue is how the image became a sort of Rorschach test in which people saw their assumptions, hopes, and fears reflected back at them. Whether or not the Obama Joker meme was originally intended to evoke racism, it soon became equated with racism by simply being deemed racist in the news media. To be sure, it was only one of many digital photo manipulations of Obama's image for use in popular Internet memes, both negative (i.e., adding a Middle Eastern turban on his head suggesting a connection to Islam) and positive (i.e., depicting his smiling face over an "Everyone chill out, I got this" slogan).

In her 2015 study of trolling, Humboldt State University's Whitney Phillips discusses the popularity of the Joker meme in online abuse and harassment. "Trolls had the most fun with the film's first official advertisement, in which the Joker traces a bloody outline of the now-infamous catchphrase, 'Why so serious?' echoing the trolling maxim that nothing should be taken seriously. 'Why so serious?' quickly entered the trolling lexicon and inspired a slew of spin-offs. Everyone from Sarah Palin to then-candidate Barack Obama was given the 'Joker treatment,' and jokerized images of cats, babies, and cartoon characters abounded" (Phillips 2015, 99). Phillips notes, "The first piece of the Obama as socialist Joker puzzle is trollish engagement with Christopher Nolan's *The Dark Knight*. Not only did the publicity surrounding Heath Ledger's death—the actor overdosed shortly after the film wrapped—imbue his Joker character with an acute, almost ironic morbidity, trolls on [messageboard] 4chan/b/ identified with his character's seemingly motiveless pursuit of chaos. They were so taken by Ledger's Joker, in fact, that they collectively adopted him as /b/'s unofficial mascot." For more on clown trolls see chapter 13.[1]

These activists who use Ronald McDonald and the Joker in their provocative art are imbued with a certain artistic legitimacy. Others don't necessarily use clown iconography in their work (some would call it performance art, others would use less kind adjectives) but instead adopt the character and techniques of clowns.

Class Clowns, Pranksters, and Hoaxers

The "class clown" is a common fixture in most classrooms and schools across the country and around the world. Loved by fellow students and often loathed by exasperated teachers, the class clown is a mild form of the bad clown—especially when defying authority—though his (it's usually a male) youthful antics are mischievous and rarely malicious. The goal of the classroom cutup is rarely to harm the teacher but instead to gain the admiration and respect of their fellow students with rude jokes, double entendres, and sight gags.

Most class clowns eventually grow out of the behavior but a few defiantly and gleefully embrace it into adulthood, trading teachers for other authority figures as targets of their subversive mirth. Freed from the confines of a single classroom or school, these bad clowns tread onto a much larger stage, that of their neighborhoods and major cities, even in some cases making international news for particularly outrageous stunts and pranks.

Two examples of prominent professional pranksters are Joey Skaggs and Alan Abel. Though not bad clowns in the strictest sense (nor evil, though their critics and targets often disagree), their work embodies the clown character in modern America. These clowns often run afoul of not only polite society but also, on occasion, the law.

New York City artist Joey Skaggs is one of the pioneer practitioners of what would become "culture jamming," a term that Kalle Lasn would adopt for his 2000 counterculture book *Culture Jam: How to Reverse America's Suicidal Consumer Binge—And Why We Must*. One of Skaggs's best-known hoaxes began with a 1976 advertisement in the *Village Voice* offering a "Cathouse for Dogs featuring a savory selection of hot bitches. From pedigree (Fifi, the French Poodle) to mutts (Lady the Tramp). Handler and vet on duty. Stud and photo service available." Skaggs ended with a phone number for interested parties to call, along with the prophetic disclaimer "No weirdos, please."

Skaggs wrote up a press release touting his fictional canine-pleasuring business, and as he said in an interview, "The response was unbelievable. I had people willing to pay fifty dollars to have their dog sexually gratified" along with a selection of people who he had explicitly asked not to contact him. Encouraged by the reaction, Skaggs hired two dozen actors to stage a performance titled "A Night in a Cathouse for Dogs" and invited the news media to cover it. This led to an in-depth interview with ABC News about the dubious enterprise, with the reporter dutifully contacting a second source for commentary: the American Society for the Prevention of Cruelty to Animals. According to Skaggs the ASPCA "sent armed investigators to get me. They put up a reward poster in my hallway offering a $200 reward for anyone who would turn me in for abusing animals. The police were calling . . . and I was subpoenaed by the Attorney General for illegally running a cathouse for dogs" (Juno and Vale 1987, 40).

Countless news-media outlets picked up the "too good to check" story, and the ABC News documentary on the Cathouse for Dogs—complete with Joey Skaggs as a pimp for canines—was nominated for an Emmy for Best Newscast of the Year. The hoax was finally revealed when Skaggs appeared before the Attorney General's office and explained that it had all been a piece of performance art designed to increase media literacy, an experimental look at "the ethics and responsibility of investigative journalists. When we are dependent upon the media for objective truth and we are not getting it, and when it's intentionally not told to us, that's disinformation, deceit, and it's blatantly irresponsible" (Juno and Vale 1987, 40). While some news media grudgingly ran follow-up stories admitting they'd been duped, according to Skaggs, ABC News never retracted or corrected its story.

Like many clowns—and Internet trolls—Skaggs also skewered politically correct conventions long before it was fashionable to do so. In 1982 Skaggs took up the cause of the Gypsies, demanding that the gypsy moth be renamed so as not to further malign the reputations of the perpetually oppressed Romany. Skaggs, as "Jo-Jo, the King of the New York Gypsies," held a protest outside the governor's office holding up a sign that demanded, "Rename the Gypsy Moth" and "Gypsies Against Stereo-typical Propaganda." Skaggs earnestly pleaded to passersby to call the gypsy moth anything else that's bad—even the "Hitler moth," because "we Gypsies have taken enough abuse." Even in those days—decades before manufactured outrage would become a common tool to get attention in the sea of pseudonews generated by the modern news cycle—some reputable news outlets sensed a hoax and chose not to report the story. The *New York Times* was not among them.

Another bad clown in a similar vein is Alan Abel, who circulated a petition at the 2000 Republican National Convention urging Americans to ban breastfeeding. It read in part, "This primitive ritual has and continues to be a violation of babies' civil rights. It's an incestuous relationship with mothers leading to moral decay. Women enjoy an erotic experience that imposes oral gratification on innocent infants after birth. Their reprehensible behavior teaches children illicit sex, subsequently manifesting addiction to promiscuity. Republicans: choose a candidate who supports our cause!" The story circulated widely but was eventually revealed to be a hoax by the media-savvy David Mikkelson of the Snopes website (Mikkelson 2007). Abel explained that his goal was "to shake people up—give them a verbal or visual kick in the intellect, so they are able to suddenly stop and look at themselves and laugh more" (Juno and Vale 1987, 107). This laughing-but-serious role of satirizing human foibles and holding a mirror up to society is that of the clown through and through.

Though the most notable pranks by Skaggs, Abel, and their contemporaries occurred in the 1970s and 1980s, their work has been continued by others such as the media-hoaxing duo the Yes Men (subject of the documentary films *The Yes Men, The Yes Men Fix the World*, and *The Yes Men Are Revolting*). Street artists such as San Francisco's Craig Baldwin hijacked and defaced advertising billboards, repurposing their existing imagery (such as brand names, slogans, and corporate logos) to make social justice and anticonsumerist statements, and the members of the Biotic Baking Brigade have for years thrown pies in the face of those they accuse of economic fascism and social injustice, including Bill Gates and Ann Coulter.[2]

These pranks and stunts are a provocative mix of performance art, social commentary, hoaxing, and satire—the same tools used by clowns for centuries. These clowns and clown theme–using artists tend to be idiosyncratic and independent. Though trying to make points about social justice issues they usually work alone and perform alone and in secret (at least until the time comes to reveal the artwork or hoax). There is another type of activist clown, one whose targets are not typically multinational conglomerates but instead friends and neighbors. They operate as part of a community, usually as part of a group helping to keep order and dispense a form of social pressure and justice. These are Native American clowns.

Native American Clowns

Though Native American clowns have a strong trickster element—as the examples here demonstrate—few can truly be accurately characterized as bad or evil. Roger Herring, writing in the *Journal of Multicultural Counseling and Development*, notes that "the clown motif exists in almost every Native American Indian culture of North America but it is especially emphasized in the Southwest. . . . Clowns, as a group, represent the rise of a unique sort of individuality in Native American Indian cultures, possessing the extraordinary power, the privilege, the license, and the expressive freedom denied other tribal members" (Herring 1994, 153). This can range from the truth-telling function common to court jesters to silly antics that would otherwise be frowned on as disruptive; for example, "Plains Indian clowning takes the form of 'contrary' behavior, such as talking or performing actions backward and in other ways violating natural and social conventions" (Miller Van Blerkom 1995, 463).

HOPI AND NAVAJO CLOWNS

Clowns often serve as intermediaries between Indians and their deities. For example

> To-ne-ni-li, Water Sprinkler, is an important character in Navaho mythology. He is a rain god. In the dry paintings of the Navaho rites he is shown as wearing a blue mask bordered with red, and trimmed on top with feathers. Sometimes he is represented carrying a water pot. In the rite of *kledzi hatal*, during the public dance of the last night, he is represented by a masked man who enacts the part of a clown. While other masked men are dancing, this clown performs various antics according to his caprice. He walks along the line of dancers, gets in their way, dances out of order and out of time, peers foolishly at different persons, or sits on the ground, his hands clasped across his knees, his body rocking to and fro. At times he joins regularly in the dance; toward the close of a figure, and when the others have retired, pretending he is unaware of their departure, he remains going through his steps. Then, feigning to suddenly discover the

absence of the dancers, he follows them on a full run. Sometimes he carries a fox skin, drops it on the ground, walks away as if unconscious of his loss; then, pretending to become aware of his loss, he turns around and acts as if searching anxiously for the skin, which lies plainly in sight. He screens his eyes with his hand and crouches low to look. Then, pretending to find the skin, he jumps on it and beats it as if it were a live animal that he seeks to kill. (Matthews 1994, 230)

With only slight differences this basic routine can be seen reflected in the antics of circus clowns around the world—the slapstick, the misdirection, the feigned stupidity is universal.

Among the Hopi,

Every village of these disparate people can have performances by at least one group of sacred clowns. If asked about the nature of these clowns and why they exist, most Pueblo people will maintain a strict silence, or give the stock answer that they are only for amusement. When Hopi are asked about the importance of the clowns, their actions, and their purpose, the explanation depends upon the position and the age of the one who answers. The elders or chiefs justify clowning by saying, "They are worth something. They do it for rain, crops, fertility," Others, somewhat younger and often more acculturated, will express a humanistic philosophy with the statement, "The clowns represent ourselves. They do all the things we do. They act like children. They don't know how to behave." (Matthews 1994, 2)

As with other activist clowns there is of course a deeper social purpose to the antics: "The underlying drive to maintain cultural cohesion and preserve the status quo." Part of the Hopi clown's role is to call attention to "any deviant behavior, whether that of strangers and their idiosyncrasies, or more importantly, problems within the village, [which] is grist for the clown's performance. All forms of humor are used, with mockery and caricature being the clowns' main method of ridiculing any transgression of accepted social mores" (Matthews 1994, 3).

It is interesting to note that this is similar to the method used by dip clowns (see the next chapter), though for different purposes. The Hopi clowns taunt and mock to nudge errant people into social conformation and proper behavior (arguably the opposite of many other activist clowns who encourage rejection of social conformity), while the dip clowns taunt and mock people for money, but also for entertainment. Parallels to the dip clowns are clear: "There is an inordinate fear on the part of the individual of having one's shortcomings exposed to village scrutiny through the activities of the clowns," just as passersby on the midway do their best to stay out of the line of sight of the dip clown lest their shortcomings be publicly mocked. Of course the target of the Hopi clowns are often (though not always) other members of the community, while dip clowns have no personal connection to those they insult.

The role of Native American clowns as agents of social control is well illustrated by this example:

> The Piptuyakyamu [a type of Hopi clown] portrayed the marital difficulties of a young Hopi man who had married a Navajo girl. He brought his new wife home but their marriage was rocky, and their problems echoed throughout the village at night. When the Piptuyakyamu appeared during the next kachina dance, they proceeded to enact all of the problems of the young couple in full view of the rest of the villagers. The hilarity that accompanied this episode indicated how close to the mark the Piptuyakyamu were in their skit. Almost certainly the couple's actions and arguments were on a far quieter plane thereafter. (Matthews 1994, 103)

These and other clown routines share many common features. For example both the clowns and the spectators are part of a social contract that allows such boorish behavior as performance. Clowns are given latitude and license to break the rules of social etiquette for our entertainment and for the greater good.

CLOWNS AS SHAMANS

The link between clowns, shamans, and quasi-supernatural trickster figures is perhaps clearest in Native American clowns. "Most pre-literate cultures have clowns who behave in a manner similar to the jester, giving unsolicited advice through the medium of humor. However, the role of these [Hopi] clowns is far more complex that than of the court fool because, in addition to offering humor and advice, they are often believed to be quasi-inhabitants of the supernatural world or to personify beings from there. Such clowns are therefore sacred and are a combination of jester, priest, and shaman" (Matthews 1994, x).

Cheryl Carp, writing in *The Arts in Psychotherapy*, notes that

Native Americans of the Southwest . . . hold the trickster in high regard. He/she is symbolized in Pueblo culture by the *kachinas*, also known as sacred clowns or funny faces. Jamake Highwater, in his book, *Ritual of the Wind* (1984), writes that the sacred clown is a "cosmic contrary," the apotheosis of paradox. He/she possesses great power, holding in balance the divine and the profane. The clowns' irrational, irreverent antics during ceremonies serve as proof of their knowledge of and connection to a divine reality. Highwater writes that the clown's freedom and perversity is a manifestation of its spirituality. Through ritual and ceremony the sacred clown functions for the community as a connection with the gods. During the Ceremony of the Rain Powers of San Juan Pueblo in New Mexico, the clowns are the only ones able to understand and speak with the rain gods. They translate the gods' message for the people. The clowns also have the freedom to make fun of and laugh at the gods, even going so far as to ridicule their position of power and send them back to their homes. The clowns serve to bring the gods to a human level; they act as irreverent ambassadors between the temporal and spiritual worlds. (Carp 1998, 247)

Ordinary circus clowns may not be associated with "real" magic, the supernatural, or spiritual communion the way that Native American clowns are, though it's not a far leap, even in oversize shoes. A clown is supposed to be a benevolent character, but anyone who has—or seems to have—magical or quasi-magical abilities (such as having a rose that squirts water or producing a bouquet of flowers from thin air) may be suspect.

Shamans, like witch doctors and others traditionally associated with magic, are often thought of as good and benevolent, but can also be evil and malevolent. The same gifts and powers that can heal or bless can also harm or curse. This idea can be seen in the distinction made between good (or "white") magic and bad (or "black") magic; as Brian Levack notes in his comprehensive survey of witchcraft during the Middle Ages, "The distinction between black and white magic can easily become blurred, especially when magicians harm someone in order to protect themselves, or when they cure someone by transferring the disease to another person. Acts of love magic very often fall into this gray area, since one person's gain in love might easily be another's loss" (Levack 2006, 6). If an anonymous clown can do the seemingly impossible—through legerdemain or packing a dozen colorful compatriots in a gimmicked car apparently the size of a couch—it's not surprising that we may wonder what they might do if angered or vindictive. Putting curses on people and turning them into toads is witches' work, but clowns may have similarly nasty things up their baggy sleeves along with those colorful hankies.

PLATE 1. *Bizarro* © 2014 Dan Piraro, distributed by King Features. Reprinted by permission.

PLATE 2. A crucified clown dies for our collective sins on the cover of *Caliber Presents* comic, art by John Bergin. From the author's collection.

PLATE 3. Cackles the Clown Halloween mask, manufactured by Gemmy Industries and sold in Atlanta, Georgia, September 2014. Photograph by the author.

PLATE 4. The Joker, the murderous Clown Prince of Crime, on a child's toy. From the author's collection, photograph by the author.

PLATE 5. A knife-wielding clown stalks a woman pretending to write something on a piece of paper outside a circus tent on the cover of the May 1962 issue of *Official Detective Stories*. From the author's collection.

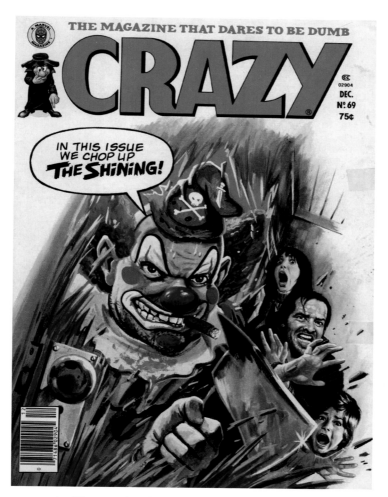

PLATE 6. Obnoxio the clown satirizes a famous scene from *The Shining* on the cover of the December 1980 issue of *Crazy* magazine. From the author's collection.

PLATE 7. Frenchy the Clown entertains kids with a wholesome campfire tale on the cover of *Evil Clown Comics* in the September 1991 issue of *National Lampoon*. From the author's collection.

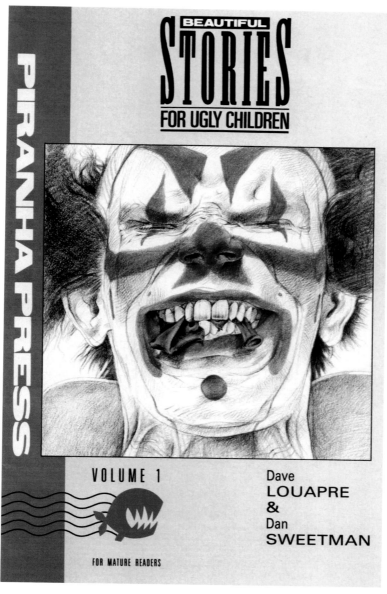

PLATE 8. A gang of clowns and freaks goes on a road trip following a circus fire in *Beautiful Stories for Ugly Children*, published by Piranha Press. From the author's collection.

PLATE 9. The demonic Clown from the *Spawn* series 20 (Classic II), issued by McFarlane Toys in 2001. From the author's collection.

PLATE 10. The original evil-clown doll used in the film *Poltergeist* (1982), on display at Planet Hollywood in Las Vegas, Nevada. Photograph by Celestia Ward, used by permission.

PLATE 11. Poster advertising the film *Killer Klowns from Outer Space* and its soundtrack performed by the Dickies. From the author's collection.

PLATE 12. Disgruntled Spanish clown Javier is upset—possibly because a cafe stopped serving breakfast—in *The Last Circus* (2010). Warner Bros./Magnet publicity still.

PLATE 13. Killer clown Pennywise from the *It* television miniseries (1990), featured on a signed collector's item photograph. From the author's collection.

PLATE 14. Promotional insert featuring *The Damn! Show*'s Yucko the Clown offering a thankfully faux "scratch and sniff" opportunity to smell the clown's "stinky hole." From the 2005 DSP LLC/ StudioWorks Entertainment DVD release of *Yucko the Clown in The Damn! Show*. From the author's collection.

PLATE 15. Promotional poster for the 2014 season of *American Horror Story: Freak Show*. From the author's collection.

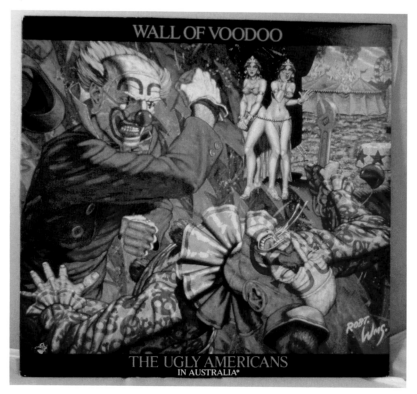

PLATE 16. Wall of Voodoo's 1988 album *The Ugly Americans in Australia,* featuring cover art by Robert Williams. From the author's collection.

PLATE 17. Ouchy the S&M Clown, who says that in his line of work "having a sadistic streak definitely helps." Publicity photograph by Glenn Campbell, used by permission, www.glenncampbellphoto.com.

PLATE 18. *Voir Dire Tragedy in One Act; Or, Judicial Review of Public Access Clown Self-Abuse* (2015). Artist's interpretation of Crotchy the Clown's obscenity trial for public-access masturbation. Illustration by Celestia Ward of Two Heads Studios. (Alternate catalog title: *Springtime in Paris*.)

PLATES 19a AND 19b. The clown that briefly terrified Staten Island residents in 2014. Photos courtesy of Fuzz on the Lens productions and used by permission.

PLATE 20. John Wayne Gacy's self-portrait as Pogo the Clown appeared on the 1994 Acid Bath album *When the Kite String Pops*. From the author's collection.

PLATE 21. George W. Bush and Osama bin Laden as clowns of death and destruction. 2010.54.5275. Chuck Sperry, *Machine Gun in the Clown's Hand*, circa 2004. Offset lithograph, 16.625 x 23.5 in. Collection of the Oakland (CA) Museum, All of Us or None Archive. Gift of the Rossman family. Reprinted by permission.

PLATE 22. The author redeems his sullied honor by dunking a dip clown at the New Mexico State Fair in 2014. Photograph by Shana Pedroncelli.

PLATE 23. Phantom clowns. Illustration by James Black.

CHAPTER 11

Crazed Caged Carny Clowns

There's a peculiar category of real-life bad clown that straddles the line between public entertainment and sadistic abuse. They are nasty, insulting, and paid pretty well by the standards of their peers. They are carnival clowns, better known as dip clowns. If you've been to a state fair or carnival you've likely seen them: clowns perched on a metal or wooden seat just above a tank of water who dare and insult passersby to dunk them—for a few bucks, of course.

Evolution of the Dip Clown

To understand where the dip clown came from and his role in the pantheon of bad clowns, it's important to have a sense of the history of the game, and to get that, I interviewed Cheyene Bere at the Erie County Fair. Bere is a pure carny, with muddy tattoos, a ruddy complexion, a discernable distrust of academics and authors, and an encyclopedic knowledge of sideshows and midways. "It was first known as the African Dip," says Bere. "They'd take a Black guy and put a grass skirt on him. They put bamboo around the tank—back then it was built like a huge kettle—put him up there, and dressed him up as a witch doctor. He wore the skirt, a bone in his nose, the whole nine yards."

The carnival game was called by many names, including the "African Dip" and "Hit the Trigger and Sink the Nigger."[1] An advertisement in the amusement and carnival catalog the *Billboard* from 1936 offered a packaged attraction called African Dip (see figure 11.1). Originally called the Cooley African Dip and manufactured by Chicago's A. M. Cooley Company, this contraption, according to the advertisement, was one of the top moneymakers at the 1933–1934 Chicago World's Fair. The illustration depicts everything the enterprising showman needs to run the joint for $125—along with a wholesome scene of a crowd watching a nattily dressed white fellow try to dunk a precariously balanced "African" into the water tank.

David Pilgrim, curator of the Jim Crow Museum in Big Rapids, Michigan, provides insight into the game's development:

> Before the Civil Rights Movement, it was not uncommon to see African Americans used as targets in carnival shows. A popular version was the game "African Dip." A Black person, usually a man, would sit on a plank and yell insults—some racial—at the White customers. The game's owner encouraged Blacks hired as 'Africans' to verbally taunt Whites; thereby ensuring long lines of angry, paying customers. The insulted White customers would try to hit a target device attached to the plank. When the target was hit squarely it caused the Black man to be dumped in the tank below. Typically, a huge crowd, some inebriated, would shout encouragement to the person throwing—and shout insults at the Black man in the "cage." When a direct hit sent the Black men into the water there were shouts of joy. It was not uncommon for some Whites to throw the balls at the Black person—protected by a net or cage—instead of the painted, circular target. The African Dip target game was found in many traveling carnival shows, seashore resorts, and fairgrounds across the United States. . . . The NAACP pressured carnival officials to close the game, but the game remained a part of [Chicago's] Riverview Park entertainment until the late 1950s. (Pilgrim 2007)

"This game has been around for a long time, and in a lot of incarnations," writes sideshow historian Lee Kolozsy. "I have seen a version where a blackface clown wearing a helmet pokes his head through a hole in the wall and insults patrons who respond by trying to bean him with

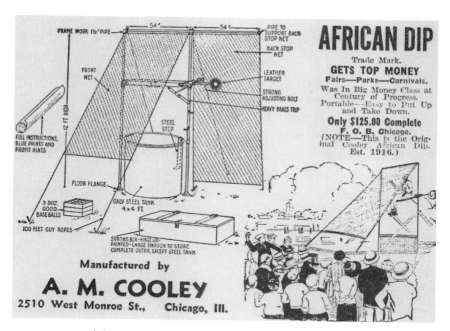

FIGURE II.I. Advertisement in the 1936 amusement catalog the *Billboard* offering an "African Dip," an early version of the modern dunk tank. From the author's collection.

hard balls. They aim for his face, and he dips his head when a strike is imminent, taking it on the helmet, which is designed to make a satisfying gong-like sound. Good showmanship, that." Kolozsy shared a similar story about a dip-clown friend of his named Bubba (not his real name— or maybe it is): on a midway one summer evening as Bubba spitfired insults at the crowd, he spied an African American gentleman. Sensing there was hay to be made from a little racist ribbing, Bubba called out, "Hey, Buckwheat! Now I remember where I know you from: your aunt is on the pancake box, and your uncle is on the rice package!" Though it's unlikely that the fellow was actually related to either an Aunt Jemima or an Uncle Ben, the taunt worked like a charm. The verbatim response— according to Kolozsy, whose reportage and understanding of dialect is surely beyond question—was: "Sheeyit! Ahm gonna sink yo' honky ass!" (Kolozsy 2003).

In some places changing social attitudes dictated a turn from racist to racy. Thus mermaids entered the dunk-tank era, lovely young ladies in seductive poses. "Coney Island had a mermaid show—A gorgeous girl would wear a mermaid's outfit," Bere explained. "The cage was much larger than they are now, and the fixed seat was replaced by a more feminine swing . . . 'Come on, big boy . . . you wanna knock me in the tank and take me home, sweetie?' She'd pull a strap down to her shoulders, give a little smile, and say she'd take more off if they knocked her in the water. . . . That was a great gag," Bere says. "Drove the guys crazy. It was popular, but didn't last too long because it was hard to hobble back onto the swing after you were dunked." A later incarnation appeared in California, with the mermaid transformed into a beauty queen, wearing a full dress and tiara. "That was so stupid," Bere said with a laugh. "She'd wreck her dress in two hours. It got too expensive to replace them."

According to Bere the modern dip clowns appeared in the early 1960s, introduced by a man named Vicki Moran. He came out with the gaudiest joint on the midway, called "Dunk Bozo in the Water"—using a generic name for the most popular clowns in the world at the time—and with that the modern dip clown was born. With the "African" no longer in vogue as a target for white balls and racial epithets, the clown took over the dunking board. Ordinary animosity against clowns—justified as it may be—wasn't enough to generate a stream of paid balls so they soon adopted the antagonizing insults borne from the African Dip.

Bere points out that dip clowns have to walk a fine line. You've got a situation involving heckling, insults, abuse, and often some form of (at least mild) intoxication on one or both sides of the cage. This robust stew of dank water, exhaustion, verbal venom, and mutual stinkeye can be combustible. "Back when I was with Vicki Moran—we sold balls real cheap back then, ten balls for three dollars—this kid who couldn't have been more than nine or ten comes onto the midway, he bought fourteen balls. It was quarter to eleven, and we closed at ten o'clock. We were the last joint open, and ready to pack it up." Bere took a long drag of his unfiltered cigarette and shook his head before shooting twin streams of smoke like a cartoon bull. "I wanted to strangle the kid. The water is cold at night, and I'm the color of my blue jeans. I'm too tired to take any more balls anyway."

Bere shakes his head in disbelief. "He must have had a magic arm or something, because he dunked me a dozen times. Up, down, up, down," he motions in the air, smoke trailing his jabs. "He should have been with the Brooklyn Dodgers. When I finally got back up, I yelled, 'High and dry, ya little bastard!'" A wide smile cracked across Bere's face and his chest puffed out ever so slightly. "Well, the crowd loved it. I got called into the office, got a $250 fine—that's some money back then—but it was worth every dime," he said with a laugh. "I'd do it again in a second."

Modern Dip Clowns: Rage in the Cage

If you think being insulted by a painted clown with a venomous tongue is rough, you should try being the clown, says David Simmons, a dip clown I interviewed at the New Mexico State Fair (see figure 11.2). Simmons got in trouble as a kid, ran away from home, and—it's a cliché, but he swears it's true—joined the carnival. "I started out as a ride jockey [mechanical ride attendant], but the ride was a piece of crap," he says. "So I told my boss, let's do the dip tank. I was joking, but she bought the tank, so I said, 'Fuck it, let's do it.' I went from throwing fat kids up rides to putting on makeup" (Simmons 2010).

He spoke to me during a break while his partner, Happy the Clown, took over the tank. Simmons, his voice raw and older than his years from calling out high-pitched insults for hours, enjoys his work but admits it's a grind. "It looks like the easiest thing in the world. But you're pulling yourself out of the water, wearing heavy clothes, the wetsuit, it gets rough. You get dunked sixty, seventy times on a good day. Or, on a bad day, four hundred times. It sucks, but every time you hit the water, you hear 'Ka-ching!'—you're making money. That's the way you gotta look at it."

As for the clown insults, Simmons echoes Bere's caution: "You gotta walk a fine line. It needs to be harsh enough to get them to buy the balls but not so bad they complain to the fair management. The first crack is the one you gotta worry about. You start out with a harsh crack—you call someone 'fat,' and when they look up, you get 'em with 'stupid.' If they're laughing, you got 'em."

Fat and *stupid* are low-hanging fruit, but much beyond that the insults often have to be carefully tailored: "You gotta know the difference

FIGURE 11.2. Dip clown David Simmons at the New Mexico State Fair in 2010. Photograph by the author.

between bikers and hippies," Simmons says. "Bikers really hate being called hippies. . . . One time in Syracuse I called to a guy, 'Hey, hippie!' and the biker ran around to the back of the tank. He tried to get into the cage, and I had to throw grease in his face. Good times . . ."

"It's the same with Mexicans, Puerto Ricans, Cubans. Unless you really know what to look for, the first couple of times you'll screw up. Mexicans hate Puerto Ricans, Puerto Ricans hate Dominicans, and Cubans hate everybody," he explains in a hard-earned cultural anthropology lesson. "If they come to the back and I'm still in the cage, I'm going in the tank. I got a ball peen hammer in there, and if you want to rush me, I'm going to bat," he says, miming Casey at the Bat with a hammer (Simmons 2010).

Simmons motions over to Happy, who's twenty yards away and reaching a fever pitch of the nasal "high and dry" in a screeching, yowling howl reminiscent of a sexually frustrated cat with a toothache. "Like Johnny, he's a small guy, and if a big guy got in there, Johnny would be finished. With me, I'm bigger, so it's when I get out of the cage that I got a problem. For some reason, you look really tiny up there. I remember one guy who was pissed off, he came around the back to confront me and I finally got mad enough to get out of the cage." The man then took measure of this wet, angry clown armed with a ball peen hammer itching to find a home in his skull and decided he wanted no part of it.

Simmons understands that he and Happy are looked down on by many of the rubes. "People laugh at us, saying how dumb we are. What they don't realize is that we're giving them nothing; maybe a few harsh words, but they're giving up a lot of money. Who's the clown really?" he asks. Bad clowns can take their tolls and hit frayed nerves, an effect Simmons is familiar with. "After people keep hearing that they're fat or ugly or whatever, after a while it's gonna piss you off. One time, I saw the guy that had the tank before us, and wow," Simmons shakes his head. "He pissed off these guys, and he was safe inside the cage because it was locked from the outside. Well, somehow they went and got bolt cutters, the clipped the lock off, and drug his ass out of the tank and beat the shit out of him. The frontman couldn't do nothing because it was an old lady, his wife. That's why it's important to have a community here, not to piss off the people you work with. Because one day you'll find yourself with four people jumping on you, and you need these guys to watch your back."

Simmons reminisced about another anticlown mob he saw: "I saw this dip clown start to get massacred by four people, and like sixty Mexicans just came and started ripping him apart. He survived, but he didn't walk right after that and [worked on] rides after that." It's not all violence and insults, though: there are bad clown groupies. Sometimes girls will flash their breasts at them, or call out to them. Simmons's employer, Lynn Meyers, added that dip clowns will often have two or three girls (sometimes as young as fifteen) hanging around afterward to meet the clowns. "One girl said she was in love with him," she said with a smile.

Schadenfreude and Social Dynamics

Aside from the early racist elements, the dip-clown joint provides an interesting social dynamic: the crowd laughs when the clown's insults hit their target in the crowd, subtly siding with the clown in a clear case of "No, we're not laughing *with* you, we're laughing *at* you." On the other hand the object of the aggressive spectacle changes when the clown is finally dunked (perhaps after many balls and many minutes): the tension is released and the crowd cheers as the bad clown gets his watery and public comeuppance. The clown quickly reclaims his seat—often with a defiant laugh or chuckle, the equivalent of a boxer smiling at his opponent just after taking a hard jab to the jaw. The cycle begins anew, with many in the crowd trying to avoid eye contact and stay inconspicuous lest they be the next target of his insults.

Most people, of course, take the act in good fun—and for those who don't there's often a sign reminding the rubes of midway dip-clown etiquette. Because the crowd is constantly moving, most people don't stay for longer than a few minutes unless a friend or family member is interacting with the clown. This allows insult material to be recycled; unlike a stand-up comic in front of the same crowd for a set, the dip clown can repeat the same lines every twenty minutes.

One of the most difficult parts of being a dip clown is keeping up the constant patter. A headlining stand-up comic only performs a set of about an hour and a half, and a singer may be on stage for two or two and a half hours. But there are very few jobs as vocally and psychologically demanding as a dip clown, who may perform more or less continuously for ten, twelve, or fourteen hours (depending on how many other clowns are available to man the booth). The dunk tank relies on the clown to lure in his antagonists, usually by identifying potentially risible people in the crowd, insulting and goading them to give it up and throw down a couple of quid.

One role of clowns has always been of the truth teller, the one who can say honest things that others are too polite or politic to speak out loud. In the realm of the dip clowns, he of course starts with a grain of truth about his victim—the knobby knees, the extra fifty pounds, the unfortunate haircut—and then expands on it like a caricaturist. Pretty much any other visible attribute is fair game; being fat (if they are), being old (if they're not), being ugly, clothing choices, and so on.

There are a few groups rarely targeted by these bad clowns, including the mentally disabled. The elderly and frail, for example, are generally left alone for the simple reason that they are unlikely to be shamed or insulted into buying baseballs. They also would not have the physical skills to hit the target, and a clown making fun of someone—who may for example be a war veteran who can't hit the target because of a war injury received defending God and country—would sour the mood and make everyone look bad. A ball peen hammer wouldn't save a clown from that crowd. Antagonizing unlikely customers is not only a waste of breath but also a poor business strategy.

Modern dip clowns are invariably men, likely because it's physically demanding work, because most insult comics are male, and because an institutionalized act of aggression toward a woman would likely be deemed too politically incorrect in today's social milieu—even for a carny midway.

Dunk N Alien

Even though many midway acts such as freak shows have been crowded out by mechanical rides, the dip clowns are still around, on midways and state fairs across the country. At the Las Vegas Pinball Hall of Fame there is a surreal and irresistible blend of Skee-Ball, dip clowns, and space-age aliens. The Dunk N Alien arcade game is essentially a Skee-Ball game that dispenses tickets, but with a twist: the goal is to hit a moving target crossing over in front of an alien figure who's insulting you.

FIGURE 11.3. Dunk N Alien game at the Las Vegas Pinball Hall of Fame. Photograph by the author.

Developed and released by Innovative Concepts in Entertainment of Clarence, New York, Dunk N Alien, as one description at i-agaming.com calls it, is "the most unique and attractive game ever manufactured by ICE. Hit a 'movable' target that will dunk a 'heckling' alien character in the back of the game. The sounds of this game are unbelievable and players keep coming back for more!" As the alien sits on his stool waiting to be "dunked" (there is of course no water involved in this electrified game), he calls out a string of insults such as "Somebody help this guy! What game are you playing? Dump the ball? Where's your glasses? Go ahead, let's go! Nah-nah-nah-nah-nah!"[2] Like a dip clown, the colorful, big-eyed alien hurls insults as players hurl rubber balls.

The game doesn't even make sense: Why would an alien heckle people into throwing balls at it, especially when—despite the name Dunk N Alien—there is nothing to dunk the alien in (not even a fake water tank with a recorded splashing sound)? Of course being taunted by a real person—who can comment about your weight, bad toupee, and dubious parentage—is more effective than a prerecorded alien voice. Nevertheless, in true dip-clown fashion the real motivator is peer pressure, and poor performance followed by an insult (whether "personal" or not) may likely carry enough weight to motivate a player to deposit another few quarters in hope of redemption.

CHAPTER 12

The Phantom Clowns

M ost evil clowns are fictional and as such reside only in our entertainment and imaginations, leaving only a handful of real flesh-
and-blood monsters that stalk our streets. We know, for example, that
Stephen King's Pennywise wasn't real, though John Wayne Gacy's Pogo
was.

Yet there is another category of bad clown, one that seems to exist
somewhere in the twilight between the cold, clear reality of daylight and
the slumbered stuff of nightmares. These bad clowns are reported to
roam streets and parks in the United States, the United Kingdom, and
elsewhere looking for innocent children to lure and abduct—yet seem to
vanish just before police can apprehend them. Some say they are real,
while others claim they are figments of imagination. They are known as
phantom clowns.

Researcher Loren Coleman coined the term and described them in the
pages of *Fate* magazine and in his book *Mysterious America*. One of the
first reports of phantom clowns occurred on May 6, 1981, when police in
Brookline, Massachusetts, issued an all-points bulletin asking officers to
watch for a vehicle containing potential child abductors. The vehicle was
distinctive: an older-model van with a broken headlight, no hubcaps, and
ladders on the side. It was also full of clowns. Several children reported
that clowns had tried to lure them into the dark van with promises of

candy, and the sinister white-faced vagabonds were later reported lurking near Brookline's Lawrence Elementary School (Coleman 1982).

It was only one in a series of mysterious threats by phantom clowns; the next day, Boston police again searched the city in vain for another van driven by a creepy clown. The man allegedly stalked nearby Franklin Park. No one else saw the clown, and despite extensive searches police once again came up empty. As reports spread to surrounding areas and parents grew nervous, Boston Public School's investigative counselor Daniel O'Connell issued a memo to principals in his school district: "It has been brought to the attention of the police department and the district office that adults dressed as clowns have been bothering children to and from school. Please advise all students that they must stay away from strangers, especially those dressed as clowns."

The New England reports soon subsided, but the clowns reappeared anew in Missouri. A sixth-grader at Fairfax Elementary School in Kansas City who saw a bad clown lurking at her school described him to the *Kansas City Star:* "He was by the fence and ran down through the big yard when some of the kids ran over there. He ran toward a yellow van. He was dressed in a black shirt with a devil on the front. He had two candy canes down each side of his pants. The pants were black too. . . . I don't remember much about his face" (Coleman 1983, 211; Callahan 1981, 7). Yet no evidence of the phantom clown could be found—not even a size-24 shoe print.

Parents were fearful, children were warned, and police were vigilant, but despite searches and police checkpoints stopping cars driven by clowns, the phantom menaces were never captured. Some people began to wonder who the clowns were, what they wanted; others wondered if they existed at all. Coleman, in a March 1982 article in *Fate* magazine, noted that "something quite unusual was happening in America in the spring of 1981. What was it? Group hysteria? Terror in the cities because of the murdered children in Atlanta? Or something else? The appearance of phantom clowns in the space of one month in at least six major cities spanning over 1,000 miles of America constitutes a genuine mystery" (Coleman 1982, 55).

While some dismissed the clown scare as a silly hoax or the product of imaginative children, many people took it seriously. One poster on the

Unsolved Mysteries website wrote: "The denizens of the netherworld have apparently dreamed up a new nightmare to shock us. The cosmic joker is alive and well and living in a clown suit! PLEASE, HELP KEEP OUR CHILDREN SAFE!" Another person suggested that the phantom clowns were actually part of a covert government conspiracy operation designed to diminish the credibility of child eyewitnesses: "Perhaps a 'clown op' was run to discredit the testimony of children . . . and lead the public toward discounting even more nightmarish mysteries" (SizeofLight 2010).

Some reporters, such as Lucinda Smith of the *Montclair* (New Jersey) *Times*, poured cold water on the stories and tried to reassure concerned parents and pupils: "Someone dressed as Homey the Clown is not in Montclair trying to hurt children. . . . And none of the following has been seen in a van attempting to kidnap children in Montclair: Homey, Krusty the Clown, the four Teenage Mutant Ninja Turtles, the Smurfs, Bugs Bunny, the Little Mermaid, Barbie, Ken" (Smith 1991).

In fact, though clowns were by far the most commonly reported threat, "there were accounts of people wearing Bart Simpson or Ronald McDonald masks or dressed as monkeys, turtles, gypsies, or policemen. The threat these bad people posed was generally not defined. There were a small handful of accounts where the candy the clowns were handing out was supposed to be drugged, or rape was hinted at, or facial cuts such as made by 'Smiley Gangs' were supposedly inflicted, or where children said they would be chopped up and put in a deep-freeze and eaten for lunch" (Bennett and Smith 2007, 263).[1] In some variants the clowns are rumored to butcher the children and, in a Hansel-and-Gretel-meet-Sweeney-Todd twist, cannibalize their tender meat for sandwiches; others say that "the blood was sold with the ice cream as raspberry sauce to get rid of the evidence" (Hobbs and Cornwell 2001, 210).

According to folklorist Jan Brunvand, "The phantom-clowns tradition involving vans seems to be exclusively a part of child lore, perhaps reflecting children's actual distrust and even fear of clowns, who, ironically, are thought by adults to be invariably amusing to youngsters, most of who would undoubtedly prefer a large, friendly, purple dinosaur to a clown any day" (Brunvand 2001). Rumors of the phantom clowns were published in several newspapers, including the Newark *Star-Ledger* and the

Boston Globe. While newspapers were the primary source for information about the fearsome clowns, warnings also circulated through informal local and regional outlets. For example, one newsletter sent to parents and teachers in 1986 warned that clowns were responsible for innocent children being "spirited away to join the throngs of missing children whose pathetic faces peer at us from milk cartons, shopping bags, and telephone [posts]" (Brunvand 1991). Those who circulated the rumors and warning stories were almost certainly doing so out of genuine concern for children; even if they doubted the phantom clowns were real, it was better to be safe than sorry.[2]

Stories of the child-abducting phantom clowns were not merely an invention of the news media; indeed, several children reported firsthand abduction attempts. One boy told police that he had been confronted by a clown armed with an Uzi machine gun in one hand and machete in the other. The clown fired off five shots, but the boy counterattacked the surprised clown by throwing his book bag at him. Deciding that an Uzi and a machete were no match for a small bag of schoolbooks, the clown then ran off. Not surprisingly, the boy later admitted that he had made up the whole story, but his reported encounter with the fearsome clown was only one of many similar reports circulating in schoolyards. According to Brunvand, "New Jersey police questioned 700 schoolchildren, many 'petrified' by the rumors, but concluded, 'We couldn't substantiate the existence of a clown. We have no sightings, no assaults, no homicides.'" An East Orange police officer described the panic: "It just spread from one kid to another, and continued until there was a kind of hysteria" (Brunvand 1991).

Whether they were observations of "real" phantom clowns or mass hysteria, reports surfaced once again in 1995 in the Central American country of Honduras, where "killer clowns" were said to be cruising the streets of large cities such as Tegucigalpa and San Pedro Sula in cars or ambulances, abducting children (Bennett 2005, 199). The phantom clowns disappeared for more than a decade, until sightings plagued Chicago, Illinois, in October 2008. According to researcher Loren Coleman, "a man wearing clown make-up and a wig was using balloons in an attempt to lure children into his vehicle on the South Side of Chicago, Illinois. The man, who wears a clown mask or white face paint with teardrops on the cheek, has approached children walking to and from school, police said. Witnesses told police he was seen driving a white or brown van with the windows broken out" (Coleman 2008). The first two incidents were reported on October 7 and 10; two days after the second incident, police held a press conference stating that there had been multiple sightings of the phantom clowns at various places around Chicago. Brunvand summarizes that "a mini-scare of killer-clown stories surfaced briefly in Phoenix, Arizona, in 1985, and the rumors returned in full force again in 1991 with reports ranging from New Jersey to Chicago and often likening the alleged threatening figure to the character Homey the Clown from the TV series *In Living Color*" (Brunvand 2012, 484).

In each case the phantom-clown sightings followed a predictable pattern: police followed up on sightings but developed no leads, and as always no arrests were made; it seemed the evil would-be abductor clowns simply vanished.

Phantom Clowns Return

Though the 1980s and 1990s were the heyday of phantom-clown sightings, they continued into the new century. In October 2008,

> several children in various districts of Chicago reported being approached by a man wearing clown makeup and a wig, carrying balloons and attempting to lure them into his car. Incidents were reported in the city's south side on 7 October (South Mackinaw Avenue) and 10 October (South Normal Avenue); subsequent reports included two on 15 October from the Hyde Park neighborhood near Kenwood Academy and at 75th Street and South Shore Drive. While police were taking the reports seriously, a spokesman said that past scares involving men dressed as clowns "cast some doubt on some of the current claims." Two reports from the city's west side were believed to be bogus. (*Fortean Times* 2009)

The phantom-clown reports resurfaced in Scotland in the early 1990s; one parent reported that "a rumor was going round—someone, a person or people, dressed in a clown's outfit, going around in a blue van giving sweets to children.... [However] my son who is eleven and my daughter who is eight ... told me that in fact there were three individuals going round, one with a Bart Simpson mask, one with a Ronald McDonald mask, and one with a turtle mask. They were driving around in a van that was disguised as a police van, throwing out bags of sweets to children, and that in fact the sweets were drugged" (quoted in Hobbs and Cornwell 2001).[3] This is of course the iconic Stranger Danger story of strangers with candy. According to Brunvand,

> Killer clown rumors surfaced briefly again in 1985, then faded until June 1991—exactly ten years after the first cycle of similar stories. . . . My first report of the return of the phantom clowns came in a letter from West Orange, New Jersey, postmarked June 12: "My mom teaches school in South Orange, and the kids at school are all terrified by the rumor that there is someone dressed as a clown driving around kidnapping children. The story has grown to the point where the clown has a name, Homey, and now they are saying that there are a whole bunch of clowns riding around in a van." (Brunvand 1991)

From Where Come the Clowns?

The first clue to solving the riddle of the phantom clowns is noting that only young children reported seeing them; adults almost never encountered them. According to a spokesman for the Boston Police Department, "No adult or police officer has ever seen a clown. We've had calls saying there was a clown. We've had calls saying that there was a clown at a certain intersection and we happened to have police cars sitting there, and the officers saw nothing. We've had over twenty calls on 911. When the officers get there, no one tells them anything" (Taylor 1981). Throughout the bad clown panic, no hard evidence was ever found, and no children were actually abducted. This strongly suggests that some form of social delusion or mass hysteria was at play. If the clowns were real, why were they so invariably incompetent? Surely at least *one* of the bad clowns would have succeeded. Any real clown could easily abduct a child at a birthday party and spirit the victim off to a waiting van. Despite the scary rumors, it seemed that the phantom clowns were as harmless to children as Bigfoot or the Boogeyman—and for the same reason.

Amid all the strange reports, police detectives, school counselors, psychologists, and others were confounded by one simple basic question: Whether they were real or not—and it was looking more and more like they were not—where did these scary clowns come from? Why would children in different places start reporting these phantom clowns?[4]

With no arrest, no suspects—and perhaps most importantly, no children actually abducted or harmed in any way—the police had nothing to go on. Many parents and school officials wondered if some of the children were simply describing creepy clowns they saw in films or on television—though the film *Killer Klowns from Outer Space* wasn't released until 1988 and thus could not have sparked or influenced any of the sightings before then; similarly, the hugely influential TV miniseries *It* didn't come out until 1990. It's possible that some of the reports during and after 1988 were influenced by these media images—and a child need not have actually seen the film to know and describe what a scary clown therein looked like because of images of film posters, advertisements, and publicity photos printed in newspapers and magazines.

Where police and others failed, folklorists such as Sandy Hobbs and David Cornwell helped supply the answer: "How did this rumor of evil clowns originate? Many of our informants suggest possible origins of the clown story: parents, police, and the mass media are all cited. One student reports that older children told the stories to frighten younger ones. Others appear to assume that the story derives from an actual incident, even though it may have become exaggerated in the telling" (Hobbs and Cornwell 2001, 212). As for what triggered the sightings, various explanations ranged from recent public safety messages featuring a clown to rental vans owned by a local company, which were blue (as in many of the bad clown reports) and featured a clownlike juggler logo on its side. Furthermore some of those blue vans had recently been used by workers in head-to-toe protective clothing that, though not distinctively clownlike, is obviously adult men whose faces and bodies are covered—oddly and perhaps menacingly to a small child's eyes. Ultimately, Hobbs and Cornwell conclude, "Searching for single causes in such cases seems unlikely to be fruitful, especially as stories about threatening clowns are older and more widespread than such explanations would suggest" (Hobbs and Cornwell 2001, 212).

Phantom clowns are best understood as part of a larger social phenomenon known as phantom attackers. These are mysterious figures, usually male and dressed in some distinctive way, and who are seen and reported as menacing ordinary citizens in public. Examples include the "Monkey Man" panic in May 2001 in which residents of New Delhi, India, claimed to have seen a sort of half-human, half-monkey creature that scared and startled people before leaping away (for a firsthand account of the panic see Edamaruku 2001); Spring-Heeled Jack, the mysterious dark-cloaked figure reported threatening and scaring people (mostly women and children) in London from the 1830s through the 1870s; the Phantom Slasher of Taiwan, who was reported stalking the streets of Taipei in 1956 trying to slash people (again, mostly women and children) with a razor; and the Mad Gasser of Mattoon, claimed to have been seen in the small eastern Illinois town in 1944 skulking outside of homes and spraying an unknown, temporarily paralyzing gas on their occupants.[5]

Though the details and descriptions vary in these cases, they have much in common, including that they all had sincere eyewitnesses who reported their encounters to police and other public safety officials; the cases were reported in the local news and residents took action to protect the public from further attempted "attacks"; the reports appeared in a given community suddenly but soon faded away with no arrest or resolution; the strange attackers were sighted but never caught, somehow always escaping just before authorities arrived; and there was no hard evidence that they ever existed in the first place—no photographs, no videotapes, no item or piece of clothing left by these scary phantoms, no nothing. In the end all these phantom attackers—like the phantom clowns—were thoroughly investigated and eventually determined not to have existed (although inevitably some mystery-mongering websites, books, and TV shows insist that they were real and possibly related to ghosts or Pennywise-like interdimensional entities).[6]

There were several other possible sociological contributors to the phantom-clown panic, including that much of it occurred a time when a moral panic gripped America in the form of sensational (and later disproven) child-abuse cases claimed to have been connected with Satanism and satanic ritual abuse. At the Fells Acres Day Care Center in Malden, Massachusetts, for example, at least one child reported that he and others had been tortured by a "bad clown" in a "secret room." Later investigation revealed that in virtually all of the cases the abuse never actually happened. There was also a series of at least two dozen high-profile child murders in Atlanta between 1979 and 1981 when the phantom-clown reports first appeared; a serial killer named Wayne Bertram Williams was later convicted of the crimes.

The phantom clowns, as folkloric entities, eventually appeared in connection with other rumors and urban legends. As folklorist Gillian Bennett notes, in the mid-1990s "people dressed as clowns were featured in rumors and panics about children being abducted for their organs in Central America; reports were circulating in Britain about bogus social workers;[7] in Belgium there were rumors of 'phantom photographers'; and in Italy rumors spread about gypsy women trying to catch children and hide them under their skirts. But the 'Killer Clowns' panics were not quite the same. What made them different was that they were caused by an urban legend that circulated exclusively among children by word of mouth" (Bennett and Smith 2007, 262). *Fortean Times* (1996) magazine reported on several cases of rumors of kidnapper clowns in Latin America, including a story claiming that "on 2 November 1995, 60 clowns gathered in the capital of Tegucigalpa, the capital of Honduras, to burn their costumes in protest over reports of kidnappers dressed as clowns bundling children into vans." Phantom-clown reports reappeared in Kent, England, shortly before Halloween 2015 (see Radford 2015b) and the scare followed a similar pattern as previous episodes. It seems likely that the world has not heard the last of the phantom clowns—real or not.

CHAPTER 13

Trolls and the Future of Bad Clowns

T his book has surveyed centuries of bad clowns in just about every imaginable media. Most of the clowns are fictional, such as Harlequin, the Joker, Pennywise, and Mr. Punch; others are real-life clowns such as John Wayne Gacy, Ouchy, and dip clowns. These self-identified clowns, like circus clowns, are engaging in a performance for a specified time and for a specific goal. There is yet another type of bad clown, a uniquely modern incarnation who acts as a clown for months or years at a time, one that has only emerged in the past two decades: the troll.

Online Trolls: Bad Clowns of the Digital Age

Though not obvious at first glance, the online troll is a version of the bad clown. A universal archetype, "the trickster does exist," writes Canadian anthropologist Gabriella Coleman, "across America, across Europe, really across the world and it is not in myth but embodied in group and living practice: in that of the prankster, hacker, the phreaker, the troller" (Coleman 2010). Trickster pranksters were discussed previously; here we turn to the trollers, the abusive Internet denizens who delight in mischief and online mayhem.

Trolls are people who, almost always anonymously, delight in provoking arguments on the web for their own amusement. "Nothing should be

FIGURE 13.1. Troll clown under a bridge gleefully spreading misery. Illustration by Celestia Ward of Two Heads Studios. (Alternate catalog title: *Cybersewage Sent.*)

taken seriously" is the unofficial troll mantra, which is of course a close variation of the Heath Ledger Joker's famous question, "Why so serious?" Trolls see themselves as taboo smashers whose real message is that the online world is populated with politically correct, easily offended ninnies who should (here I politely paraphrase) "lighten up." Anything that someone else reveres or holds dear—their memory of a loved one, their religion or reputation, or anything else—is a legitimate subject to tease him or her about, often mercilessly.

Trolling victims will often respond to trolls' questions or provocative comments with sensible arguments, not realizing that they're being trolled. In many cases the troll might in fact completely agree with the views of his or her victim, who by continuing to engage in an online discussion is merely encouraging the behavior. Trolling is inherently antagonistic arguing for the sake of arguing, pissing people off simply for the fun of it. The more vile, nasty, offensive, and outrageous the comments, the more successful the troll is.

The evil clown, adopting the digital guise of a troll, is—as all tricksters are—the wise one, the disruptive character who is in control. Like clowns, both good and bad, Internet trolls revel in duplicitous manipulation. They play the fool but do so for their own ends and on their own terms.

The pratfalls, misunderstandings, and silliness seen in clown antics are not the result of stupidity or the chaos they appear to be; they are of course staged and rehearsed for maximum effect. It's a public performance, after all, under a circus tent or at a backyard party. Clowns are traditionally only found in socially circumscribed areas and in a very specific set of circumstances such as circuses, sideshows, and parties. Troll clowns violate this expectation of boundaries by showing up in your own home via the Internet. The invasion is not a physical one, of course, but for many people who spend much of their lives online, the intrusion of this bad clown is just as real as any other.

Trolls engage in a similar performance, and in the most public place possible: the Internet. They tease or incense, outrage or amuse, depending on their whim and thirst for sadism. Clowns usually match wits with one another and with their audiences—sometimes politely (as with circus clowns) and sometimes rudely (as with dip clowns). Troll clowns follow the same pattern; their audience is not only themselves and fellow trolls but the countless nameless and faceless others who lurk and participate in social media. The troll clown is inherently malevolent; a circus clown might gently surprise or scare a kid with an unending supply of quarters seemingly pouring from a hitherto un-numismatized ear, whereas a troll may publicly accuse his victim of being a racist, Nazi, misogynist, or countless other grievous insults, on the flimsiest of reasons (or none at all).

Though trolls are widely despised and condemned for their abusive tactics, in their eyes they are doing good (or, at least, engaging in harmless fun) and even serving a higher moral purpose. Like Hopi clowns, dip clowns, Mr. Punch, and the court jesters before them, the troll acts as a self-appointed cultural critic, an outsider who can speak truth (or at least their version of "truth") to the public while plausibly maintaining that it's all in good fun and shouldn't be taken (too) seriously. Clown historian Beryl Hugill notes that "there is a popular feeling that freedom of speech implies support of the poor and oppressed. But many jesters used their freedom purely in their own self-interest" (Hugill 1980, 37).

Decades after media prankster clowns such as Alan Abel and Joey Skaggs suckered journalists and the public with hoaxes (see chapter 10), troll clowns gleefully goad the gullible news media into covering bogus moral panic–tinged news stories such as jenkem (a hallucinogenic inhalant drug made from fermented feces that, according to alarmist news stories spread by trolls, was widely used among school kids in 2007—don't ask!). Anthropologist Whitney Phillips notes that in conducting media pranks "the trolls knew exactly how to manipulate the news cycle, and in the process forwarded an implicit critique of the ways in which [news] media research and report the news. . . . Whether or not trolls deliberately forward political or cultural critiques, [those] political or cultural critiques can be extrapolated from the trolls' behaviors. . . . Trolls are agents of cultural digestion [and their] grotesque displays reveal a great deal about the surrounding cultural terrain" (Phillips 2015, 6–10). For better or worse, trolls reflect, and are part of, the social and cultural fabric.

Human foibles (personal, political, and otherwise) have always been grist for clowns, and trolls are no exception. While dip clowns are restricted to interactions with rubes in the midway crowds who happen to pass by their dunk tanks, troll clowns eagerly feed on the cornucopia of digital detritus ever present on the Internet. Anything written about, videotaped and uploaded, or commented on is fair game for mockery, from celebrity gaffes to tragic suicides. Anything anyone takes seriously—or expresses a strong opinion about—is troll bait. Troll clowns gleefully go for the jugular, often using the classic clown tools of improvisation, satire, and mockery.

Traditional clowns disguise their identities under fright wigs and behind greasepaint and garish clothes; troll clowns disguise their identities behind anonymous accounts and fake usernames. Unlike costumed clowns, however, trolls are not immediately identifiable as such. In fact that is their power: if the troll victims knew from the first exchange on social media that they were dealing with a troll (or "being trolled"), most would cease contact and move on. The troll is successful in part because his or her status is, at least initially, ambiguous. Differences of opinion are rampant on the Internet and often escalate to name calling with no assistance from trolls (a popular meme circulating around 2012 offered simple instructions for "How to Start an Argument Online: 1. Express an opinion; 2. Wait."). When interacting with anonymous strangers online people often assume that, by default, those they are conversing with are acting in good faith—as most people we encounter in real life are.

Online trolls are perhaps the most "visible" and influential version of the modern bad clown; in fact one could argue that the trolls are bad clowns incarnate. Though not literally clowns (they don't dress up in clown costumes—or if they do perform as clowns in their real lives, they don't announce their doubly anonymous lives) they certainly share many important aspects of bad clowns. Throughout their checkered past bad clowns alternated between being portrayed by actors (for example Harlequin in the commedia dell'arte or Tim Curry as Pennywise) or puppets (for example Mr. Punch). Hopi clowns and dip clowns are people playing bad clown roles, but troll clowns are a different breed, one that revels in ambiguity, for their maliciousness is only partly an act put on for the amusement of others. It instead borrows from the semiprofessional practical jokester, the prankster who may or may not invoke a greater social agenda as a motivation but nonetheless performs for his or her own amusement.

There is surely more that can be written about bad clowns in all their variety, but I've done my best to give these characters their dishonorable and dubious due. This book began by noting that one of the keys to the bad clown's longevity is his ability to change with the times. Clowns, jesters, tricksters, Harlequins, fools, trolls, and their ilk have been with us since the dawn of time and are eternal. The irrepressible scourge Mr. Punch, for example, remains alive and well centuries after his first appearance, though his infamy has been eclipsed by other clowns who continue to haunt our nightmares. As long as they are confined to fiction we delight in their mischievous antics and root on the buffoon bad boys—when they become real, well . . . that's a different matter.

Notes

Introduction

1. I contacted Glenn Kohlberger, president of Clowns of America International, asking for an interview or a statement about how clowns have been portrayed in the news media and popular culture. He did not respond to my request, though he was quoted as saying that "we do not support in any way, shape or form any medium that sensationalizes or adds to coulrophobia or 'clown fear.'" Though I would have liked to get a professional clown's perspective on the bad-clown phenomenon, I think it is both predictable and fairly well represented here. Bad, evil, and scary clowns are an embarrassment and distraction to professional clowns, the rotten apple in the barrel, whose ugly sight and smell casts suspicion on the rest of them. Commenting on bad clowns only legitimizes and draws attention to them, and good clowns just wish they would all go away. But good clowns should take heart in the fact that they greatly outnumber bad ones, and despite public perception, research shows that most kids—and most adults— neither hate nor fear clowns but enjoy then. This book is about the exception, not the rule.

   Professional clown organizations such as Clowns of America International (CAI) take clown ethics very seriously and do not tolerate bad clowns. To that end the CAI has published a set of Eight Clown Commandments, including the following:

   > I will keep my acts, performance and behavior in good taste while I am in costume and makeup. I will remember that a good clown entertains others by making fun of himself or herself and not at the expense or embarrassment of others; I will learn to apply my makeup in a professional manner. I will provide my own costume; I will neither drink alcoholic beverages nor smoke while in makeup or clown

costume. Also, I will not drink alcoholic beverages prior to any clown appearances. I will remove my makeup and change into my street clothes as soon as possible following my appearance, so that I cannot be associated with any incident that may be detrimental to the good name of clowning. I will conduct myself as a gentleman/lady at all times. I will do my very best to maintain the best clown standards of makeup, costuming, properties, and comedy.

Chapter 2

1. The cinematic sex and violence need not be performed by humans to trigger censorship; for example, in their 2004 satire film *Team America: World Police*, the boundary-pushing creators of the animated hit *South Park* included a scene of marionette puppets having sex, which initially earned a draconian NC-17 rating from the MPAA.

2. The 1993 Joel Schumacher film *Falling Down*, starring Michael Douglas as a laid-off defense worker who goes on a rampage during a walk across Los Angeles, offers a similar antihero who eventually lashes out against real and perceived abuses from others.

Chapter 4

1. Some writers (e.g., Dery 1999; McRobbie 2013b) have suggested that sporadic incidents of damaged or beheaded statues of Ronald McDonald and other clowns are evidence of widespread anticlown sentiment. However there seems to be no need to invoke any coulrophobic element to the vandalism, as many nonclown figures have been similarly smashed and attacked, including Bob's Big Boy restaurant statues and school mascots. These attacks seem far more likely to be simple acts of opportunistic vandalism than a coordinated effort by passionate clown haters to vent their bile.

2. Of course any "phobia" can be created by simply using a Greek or Latin stem and adding "-phobia" as a suffix, from "acetophobia" (fear of vinegar), "aerophobia" (fear of air), or "botanophobia" (fear of plants). Anyone can make up any word they like, but it doesn't make it a real word that's used by clinical professionals discussing the topic. Similarly, "homophobia," which today is widely taken to mean hatred toward homosexuals, has found wide usage despite the fact that it actually literally means "fear of sameness" and is unrelated to any sort of legitimate clinical phobia, such as arachnophobia or claustrophobia. According to one source, "It is difficult to place the origin of the term *coulrophobia* with any certainty. Not known before

the 1980s, it's based on the Greek *koulon* (limb), suggesting stilts and stilt-walking" (Weinberg 2007, 41).

Chapter 5

1. The tardy readers Obnoxio mean-spiritedly and irresponsibly singled out for public naming and shaming included Chris Kaufman of Tacoma, Washington; Miranda Pinero of Laurel Hill, North Carolina; Michael Lindsay of Winnfield, Louisiana; and Travis Homer Cane Jr. of Astoria, Oregon.

2. In an interview by Daniel Best, Kupperberg was asked about this scene: "Was any of this censored? I mean you've got him hitting a crack pipe with a, I don't know, it looks like a child prostitute in the background there." Kupperberg replied: "Oh yeah. No, that's a fully mature, but totally wasted, skanky, crack whore. Well, apparently the fright was over at that point. What can I tell you?" (Best 2007).

Chapter 6

1. In the horror-film genre, *dysfunctional* is a necessary qualifier when describing a family of serial killers.

2. Lobster Boy was Grady Stiles Jr., who was born with a condition called electrodactyly, which fused his fingers and toes together; he was a fixture in sideshows for decades until his murder in 1992.

3. Krusty is not inherently a bad or evil clown unless you count his chronic prescription-pill and alcohol abuse, or the abuse he heaped upon Sideshow Bob that led Bob to frame him for armed robbery, or his bitter cynicism, or his licensed endorsement of potentially lethal products such as Krusty Brand Imitation Gruel and the acid-spraying Krusty the Clown Alarm Clock.

4. There were hundreds of Bozos at one time or another doing different shows in different parts of the country, which complicates verifying the truth. Furthermore there seems to be no verified archival footage of the incident; the myth-debunking website Snopes.com has collected and analyzed several of what are claimed to be blooper reels containing the infamous exchange, but none are considered to be authentic.

Chapter 8

1. The television show *Family Guy* featured several short clown-porn spoofs; they can be seen at https://www.youtube.com/watch?v=HTexZKj1FgE.

Chapter 9

1. There actually was a gunman who claimed to have shouted, "I am the Joker! I'm gonna load my guns and blow everybody up" in late July 2012. It was not James Holmes but instead a man named Neil Prescott, who threatened to shoot his coworkers in a mass attack at the Pitney Bowes plant in Washington, DC, one week after the Aurora theater attack. Ironically, this bit of information linking a Batman villain to a threat of mass killings also turned out to be a reporting error; news reports later clarified that Prescott referred to himself as "a joker"—not *the* Joker: he was not dressed like the villain, nor was there any connection to Batman.

2. When the *Seattle Times* reported on this unfortunate incident it received a clown complaint.

> Michael "Mouse the Clown" Morrisey [explained] why he and other clowns were insulted. "Give 'em a break!" he wrote. "When will the public be treated to an in-depth portrayal of one of the classic art forms instead of articles and cinema productions that portray them as evil or unscrupulous?" . . . Morrisey is president of Cascade Clowns of Kirkland, a non-profit group with a membership of about three dozen. He is 40, and when not clowning works in title insurance. . . . "I debated for two or three weeks about writing a letter," he said. "Then I finally decided to do something. We hear from kids. Some of them will say they don't like clowns. Clowns have been portrayed as unscrupulous, evil, sinister. . . . There are clowns named "Buttons" all the way across the country," Morrisey said. "Now they'll be hearing, 'Didn't he try to bump off his wife?'" (Lacitis 1991).

Chapter 10

1. The online bulletin board 4chan is populated mostly by anonymous trolls and has been described as "an incubator for early trolling culture [that] over the years has earned the dubious distinction of being deemed 'the asshole of the Internet'" (Phillips 2015, 52).

2. Abel and Skaggs come from a long tradition of counterculture social justice pranksters whose ranks include Abbie Hoffman, Jello Biafra, Paul Krassner, and Bruno Richard; for a survey of these and other pranksters see *Pranks!* by Andrea Juno and Vicki Vale, and *The Interventionists: Users' Manual for the Creative Disruption of Everyday Life*, edited by Nato Thompson and Gregory Sholette. There are, of course, many people other than self-identified

pranksters who have pulled media pranks and hoaxes to make a social statement, including magician and skeptic James Randi (who arranged for a fake
psychic healer to tour Australia, convincing many that he was the real deal
and demonstrating the news media's gullibility); mathematician Alan Sokal
(who successfully published gibberish in the academic journal *Social Text* to
show that postmodern cultural critiques need not be comprehensible to be
published); and pioneering Pakistani physicist Lamprey Da Sousa (who
between 1979 and 2006 referenced fictional characters in his textbooks to
show that few people read, much less verify, information in endnotes).

Chapter 11

1. The feral African theme had been exploited for many years in the world of
carnivals and sideshows. Indeed, at national fairs across the country in the
first half of the twentieth century "often American-born blacks were
employed to pose as 'savages'" (Bogdan 1988, 51). In his book *Freaks: We
Who Are Not As Others*, Daniel Mannix describes a pinhead (a decidedly
politically incorrect term for people who suffer from microcephaly, and
whose heads come to a small point and who are invariably handicapped)
named "Zip, the Missing Link, who died in 1926 at the age of eighty-
four—the grand old man of the sideshows. Zip was one of P. T. Barnum's
finds and, by shrewd showmanship, Barnum made him famous.... Unlike
many pinheads Zip could talk easily and well. He was, of course, captured
in Africa and wore a sort of union suit covered with fur. To accentuate his
pointed skull, Barnum had his head shaved except for a tuft of hair at the
top.... Actually, Zip was an American Negro" (Mannix 1976, 92). Zip's
name was William Henry Johnson, born around 1840 in New Jersey, and
he "had the longest successful career of any of the sideshow attractions,"
due in large part to his retrospectively racist marketing: "In an 1860 publi-
cation for the American Museum, showmen took advantage of the public's
interest in primates and introduced Johnson as 'What Is It? or the Man-
Monkey!' describing him as 'a most singular animal, which though it has
many of the features and characteristics of both the human and the brute,
is not, apparently, either, but, in appearance, a mixture of both—the con-
necting link between humanity and brute creation'" (Bogdan 1988, 136). The
newspaper comic Zippy the Pinhead, by Bill Griffith, is named for Johnson.
For more information on Johnson and other black sideshow performers
see *Early African Entertainments Abroad: From the Hottentot Venus to Africa's
First Olympians* by Bernth Lindfors.

2. Compared to the nasal whine of "high and dry, high and dry" that seems to have been finely honed by generations of dip clowns for maximum aural irritation, the alien's prerecorded taunts are positively soothing.

Chapter 12

1. In the book *Urban Legends: A Collection of International Tall Tales and Terror*, Gillian Bennett and Paul Smith discuss a similar urban legend of so-called "Smiley Gangs," groups of sadists roaming schools and streets who would corner a victim and ask him or her a question; if the person answered wrong they would be slashed with a knife or razor from cheek to cheek, creating a grotesque smile. For example, such rumors spread in south London schools in 1989 that hooligan fans of the Chelsea Football Club would catch children and demand to know which soccer team they supported; any reply other than "Chelsea" would result in an attack. The rumors resurfaced several years later in France and Holland, where the targets were terrorized women confronted and asked to choose between "a rape and a smile" (Bennett and Smith 2007, 34).

2. There were interesting parallels between the witch hunts that plagued the 1700s and 1800s and the phantom clowns. Women accused of being witches were believed to have been seduced by Satan. While a few men were accused of being witches, the vast majority were women, due in large part to sexist notions at the time that women, being deemed less intelligent and more suggestible than men, were more likely to succumb to the Devil's charms. Children, also considered less intelligent, more gullible, and therefore vulnerable, were assumed to be drawn to strangers dressed as clowns. Thus we see the durability of the idea of the innocent naif seduced by the powerful, alluring, and malevolent trickster.

3. Variations of this legend have appeared in many countries; as Gillian Bennett and Paul Smith note in their book *Urban Legends*, "In the 1970s and 1980s stories began circulating in Poland, Byelorussia, the Ukraine, Mongolia, and Russia that children were being abducted in black Volga cars and their organs taken for spare-part surgery for rich foreigners. Between 1977 and 1989 the story was so widespread, says Polish folklorist Dionizjusz Czubala, 'that you could hardly meet a Pole who was not familiar with it. It was a time of panic among children, teachers, and parents, intensified by the media'" (Bennett and Smith 2007, 127).

4. It's important not to exaggerate the extent of phantom-clown reports and panic; it's not as if tens of thousands of children across the country and

around the world suddenly claimed to have been stalked by menacing clowns in public. Though certainly many tens of thousands of children *heard* about the incidents—the phantom clowns were, after all, the subject of schoolyard rumors, parental and police warnings, and even newspaper reports—only a small percentage, probably no more than a few dozen children in all, actually claimed to have had firsthand encounters with the menacing clowns.

5. The fascinating phenomenon of phantom attackers is far too complex to discuss here; for more on this topic see *Hoaxes, Myths, and Manias: Why We Need Critical Thinking* and *The Martians Have Landed: A History of Media-Driven Panics and Hoaxes*, both coauthored by myself and sociologist Robert Bartholomew; *The London Monster: A Sanguinary Tale*, by Jan Bondeson; and *Little Green Men, Meowing Nuns and Head-Hunting Panics: A Study of Mass Psychogenic Illness and Social Delusion*, by Robert Bartholomew.

6. For example a "Dr. G. Jenkins, Ph.D., (Th.D.), M.Sc." who posts online under the name "Psiresearcher" and is founder of something called the International Consortium for Psychical Research and Paranormal Inquiry offers a paranormal theory for the origin of these phantom clowns: "As for the images of these clowns, there may be a definite paranormal answer to this, perhaps more towards a residual [ghost] haunting, whereby the 'clown' in question falls under those auspices.... However, some of them could very well fall under a trans-dimensional guideline, whereby these creatures . . . filter at various times through the 'cosmic' scheme of things, at various times and places. I have at late been immersed in Quantum Physics [*sic*], and with the new ideals [*sic*] being investigated by serious and down-to-earth physicists, anything is possible" (Jenkins 2011).

7. For more information on organ-theft urban legends see my article "Bitter Harvest: The Organ-Snatching Urban Legends" in the May/June 1999 issue of *Skeptical Inquirer* magazine, and chapter 3 in my book *Tracking the Chupacabra: The Vampire Beast in Fact, Fiction, and Folklore*. There have been ongoing rumors in the United Kingdom of unknown people posing as social workers seen attempting to examine or abduct children. These mysterious impostors, known as bogus social workers, were reported by dozens of people. According to *Fortean Times* magazine, "The first reports . . . were in January 1990, culminating in a national bogus social worker panic the following spring, when twenty-three separate police forces took part in 'Operation Childcare.' Countless thousands of

man-hours were expended as the authorities tried to track down the perpetrators, resulting in a grand total of no arrests. Eventually the police concluded they were dealing with a social panic and admitted they were treating only eighteen of more than 250 reported incidents as 'significant'" (*Fortean Times* 2011).

References Cited

Abramovich, Seth. 2014. "Professional Clown Club Attacks 'American Horror Story' over Murderous Character." *Hollywood Reporter*. October 15. Available at http://www.hollywoodreporter.com/news/professional-clown-club-attacks-american-740768.

AFP. 2014. "Teen Arrested, Another Jailed as Clown Terror Spreads in France." October 28. Available at http://en.africatime.com/tanzanie/db/teen-arrested-another-jailed-clown-terror-spreads-france.

American Psychiatric Association. 2014. *Diagnostic and Statistical Manual of Mental Disorders*. 5th ed. Washington, DC: American Psychiatric Association.

Associated Press. 1990. "Search for Clown in Shooting Death Points at Woman." *Gainesville Sun*. September 8, 6B.

———. 2008. "Jury Convicts Former Clown on Sexual Assault." March 7. Available at http://www.twincities.com/wisconsin/ci_8491658.

Bakay, Nick. 2006. Author interview. December 7.

Barker, Clive. 1997. *Clive Barker's A–Z of Horror*. Compiled by Stephen Jones. London: BBC Books.

Barkmann, Claus, Anna-Katharina Siem, Nino Wessolowski, and Michael Schulte-Markwort. 2013. "Clowning as a Supportive Measure in Paediatrics: A Survey of Clowns, Parents, and Nursing Staff." *BMC Pediatrics* 13: 166–76.

Bartholomew, Robert. 2001. *Little Green Men, Meowing Nuns, and Head Hunting Panics: A Study of Mass Psychogenic Illness and Social Delusion*. Jefferson, NC: McFarland Press.

Bartholomew, Robert, and Benjamin Radford. 2003. *Hoaxes, Myths, and Manias: Why We Need Critical Thinking*. Buffalo, NY: Prometheus Books.

———. 2012. *The Martians Have Landed: A History of Media-Driven Panics and Hoaxes*. Jefferson, NC: McFarland Press.

BBC News. 2002. "Clown Gang Hold Up Pub." July 16. Available at http://news.bbc.co.uk/2/hi/uk_news/england/2131236.stm.

Bee, Trisha. 2013. "Convicted Sex Offender to Be Released in City of Waukesha." Fox 6 News. October 22. Available at http://fox6now.com/2013/10/22/convicted-sex-offender-to-be-released-in-city-of-waukesha/.

Benet's Reader's Encyclopedia, edited by Katherine Baker Siepmann. 1987. New York: Harper Perennial.

Bennett, Gillian. 2005. *Bodies: Sex, Violence, Disease, and Death in Contemporary Legend*. Oxford: University Press of Mississippi, 199–200.

Bennett, Gillian, and Paul Smith. 2007. *Urban Legends: A Collection of International Tall Tales and Terrors*. Westport, CT: Greenwood Press.

Bere, Cheyene. 2011. Interview with the author. September 12.

Best, Daniel. 2007. "Looking Back with Alan Kupperberg: Evil Clown Comics." *20th Century Danny Boy*. October 6. Available at http://ohdannyboy.blogspot.com/2007/10/looking-back-with-alan-kupperberg-evil.html.

Bever, Lindsay. 2014. "Las Vegas Cop Killers Packed Ammo and Wore Adult Diapers as They Prepared for their 'Revolution.'" *Washington Post*. June 24. Available at http://www.washingtonpost.com/news/morning-mix/wp/2014/06/24/las-vegas-cop-killers-packed-ammo-and-wore-adult-diapers-as-they-prepared-for-their-revolution.

Bogdan, Robert. 1988. *Freak Show: Presenting Human Oddities for Amusement and Profit*. Chicago, IL: University of Chicago Press.

Bondeson, Jan. 2001. *The London Monster: A Sanguinary Tale*. Cambridge, Massachusetts: Da Capo Press.

Bradshaw, Peter. 2009. "Did They Make Barack Obama the Joker Because He Blows Up a Hospital?" *Guardian* (UK). August 19. Available at http://www.theguardian.com/film/filmblog/2009/aug/19/obama-joker-heath-ledger-poster.

Brioux, Bill. 2008. *Truth and Rumors: The Reality Behind TV's Most Famous Myths*. Westport, CT: Praeger.

Bruce, Cara. 2002. "Bedding Bozo: Fun with Clown Fetishes." October 23. *Eros zine: San Francisco Erotica*. This web page is no longer active. Originally at www.eros-guide.com/articles/2002-10-23/beddingbozo.

Brunvand, Jan Harold. 1991. "Take Away Kidnapping Clowns." *Post-Standard* (Syracuse, NY). August 5, A7.

———. 2000. *The Truth Never Stands in the Way of a Good Story*. Chicago: University of Illinois Press.

———. 2001. "The Phantom Clowns." In the *Encyclopedia of Urban Legends*. New York: ABC-CLIO, 313-315.

———. 2012. "Phantom Clowns." In the *Encyclopedia of Urban Legends*. Updated and expanded edition. New York: ABC-CLIO, 483-85.

Callahan, Christopher. 1981. "Beware 'Clown,' Pupils Told." *Boston Globe*. May 7, 21.

Campbell, Andy. 2012. "Dominic Deville, An Evil Birthday Clown, Stalks Your Child For A Fee." *Huffington Post*. May 8. Available at http://www.huffington post.com/2012/05/08/evil-clown-birthday-surprise-dominic-deville_n_ 1499369.html.

Campbell, Joseph. 1972. *The Hero with a Thousand Faces*. Princeton, NJ: Princeton University Press.

Canada Border Services Agency. 2008. "Tattoos and Their Meanings." May. Organized Crime Section. Available at https://info.publicintelligence.net/ CBSA-TattooHandbook.pdf.

Carmeli, Yoram S. 1989. "Wee Pea: The Total Play of the Dwarf in the Circus." *TDR* 33, no. 4: 128–45.

Carp, Cheryl. 1998. "Clown Therapy: The Creation of a Clown Character as a Treatment Intervention." *Arts in Psychotherapy* 25, no. 4: 247.

Carroll, Noel. 1999. "Horror and Humor." *Journal of Aesthetics and Art Criticism* 57, no. 2, 145–60.

CBSDC. 2012. "Thwarted Office Shooter Neil Prescott: 'I Am the Joker.'" July 27. Available at http://washington.cbslocal.com/2012/07/27/local-man-arrested-for-allegedly-plotting-mass-attack-on-his-coworkers/.

Chabon, Michael. 2001. "The God of Dark Laughter." *New Yorker*, April 9.

Chiodo, Edward, Stephen Chiodo, and Charles Chiodo. 2007. Interview by the author. March 18.

Chow, Denise. 2009. "Artist Behind 'Jokerized' Obama Image Revealed as Firas Alkhateeb, College Student and Chicagoan." *New York Daily News*, August 19. Available at http://www.nydailynews.com/news/politics/artist-behind-jokerized-obama-image-revealed-firas-alkhateeb-college-student-chicago-an-article-1.396760.

Coleman, Gabriella. 2010. "Hacker and Troller as Trickster." Blog post, February 7. Available at http://gabriellacoleman.org/blog/?p=1902.

Coleman, Loren. 1982. "Phantom Clowns." *Fate* 35, no. 3 (March): 53–54, 55.

———. 1983. *Mysterious America*. London: Faber & Faber, 211–15.

———. 2008. "Phantom Clowns Are Back." Available at http://copycateffect. blogspot.com/2008/10/phantom-clowns-are-back.html.

Collier, John Payne. (1929) 2006. *Punch and Judy: A Short History with the Original Dialogue*. Reprint, Mineola, NY: Dover.

Cozblah. 2013. "Crotchy the Clown's 1st Amendment Rights?" June 17. World News Forum. Available at http://www.topix.com/forum/world/ TL7QHQVBDC276E3PI.

The Damn! Show. 2005. DVD. Studio Works Entertainment.

Davies, Owen. 2009. *Grimoires: A History of Magic Books*. New York: Oxford University Press.

de la Iglesia, Álex. 2010. *The Last Circus*. DVD director's commentary. Tornasol Films.

Dery, Mark. 1999. *The Pyrotechnic Insanitarium: American Culture on the Brink*. New York: Grove Press.

Deville, Dominic. 2012. "The Real Story behind the Evil Birthday Clown (aka Dominic Deville)." Itsybitsysteps.com. May 11. Available at http://www.itsy bitsysteps.com/the-real-story-behind-the-evil-birthday-clown-aka-dominic-deville/.

Diagnostic and Statistical Manual of Mental Disorders. 2013. 5th ed. Washington, DC: American Psychiatric Association.

Douglas, John, and Mark Olshaker. 1997. *Journey into Darkness*. New York: Scribner.

Ebert, Roger.1992. *Shakes the Clown*. Film review. March 13. Available at http://www.rogerebert.com/reviews/shakes-the-clown-1992.

———. 2005. *The Devil's Rejects*. Film review. July 21. Available at http://www.rogerebert.com/reviews/the-devils-rejects-2005.

Edamaruku, Sanal. 2001. "The 'Monkey Man' in Delhi: A First-Hand Report on How the Rationalists Stopped the Mass Mania." *Rationalist International Bulletin*, no. 72, May 23.

Elliot, Ian. 2010. "Napanee Clown Arrested." *Intelligencer*. October 8. Available at http://www.intelligencer.ca/2010/10/08/napanee-clown-arrested.

Emanuel, Michael. 2014. Interview by the author. May 30.

Evans, Colin. 1996. *The Casebook of Forensic Detection: How Science Solved 100 of the World's Most Baffling Crimes*. New York: John Wiley.

Folks, Mike. 1992. "Clown Case Still Mystery After 2 Years Woman Gunned Down in Doorway of Home." *Sun-Sentinel* (Palm Beach, FL). May 26. Available at http://articles.sun-sentinel.com/1992-05-26/news/9202110190_1_marlene-warren-clown-car-dealership.

Fortean Times. 1996. "Fears of a Clown," no. 85. March, 17.

———. 2001. "Bogus Social Workers." Strange Days column, no. 270. February, 10.

———. 2009. "Scarelore," Strange Days column, no. 247. May, 16.

Gaiman, Neil, and Dave McKean. 1994. *The Comical Tragedy or Tragical Comedy of Mr. Punch*. New York: Vertigo Books.

Gibson, Jim. 2004. "No Clowning Around." *Times Colonist* (Victoria, BC). May 7, C6.

Globe and Mail. 1990. "Fear of Clowns." *Globe and Mail*. June 22, A12.

Goldhammer, Zach. 2014. "Scary Clowns Are Terrorizing France." *Atlantic*. October 31. Available at http://www.theatlantic.com/international/archive/2014/10/clown-killer-quest-ce-que-cest/382092/.

Gomez, Luis. 2014. "Haunted House Owners Share Their Opinions on John Wayne Gacy Room." *Chicago Tribune*. October 1. Available at http://my.chicagotribune.com/#section/-1/article/p2p-81558029/.

Greenberger, Robert. 2008. *The Essential Batman Encyclopedia*. New York: Del Rey.

Grewal, San. 2013. "Brampton's Clowns Need No Licence to Amuse as Council Backs Down on Regulation." *Toronto Star*. August 7. Available at http://www.thestar.com/news/city_hall/2013/08/07/bramptons_clowns_need_no_licence_to_amuse_as_council_backs_down_on_regulation.html.

Gustines, George Gene. 2010. "The Joker in the Deck: Birth of a Supervillain." *New York Times*. October 2, C2.

Henderson, Schuyler, and Katyna Rosario. 2008. "But Seriously: Clowning in Children's Mental Health." *Journal of the American Academy of Child Adolescent Psychiatry* 47, no. 9 (September): 984–85.

Herring, Roger. 1994. "The Clown or Contrary Figure as a Counseling Intervention Strategy with Native American Indian Clients." *Journal of Multicultural Counseling and Development* 22, no. 3: 153.

Hobbs, Sandy, and David Cornwell. 2001. "Killer Clowns and Vampires: Children's Panics in Contemporary Scotland." In *Supernatural Enemies*, edited by Hilda Ellis Davidson and Anna Chaudhri. Durham, NC: Carolina Academic Press.

Honan, Mat. 1999. "Crotchy the Masturbating Clown: Testing the Limits of Self-Expression." July 30. Available at http://www.gettingit.com/article/569.

Hugill, Beryl. 1980. *Bring On the Clowns*. Secaucus, NJ: Chartwell Books.

Jando, Dominique. 2008. *The Circus: 1870s–1950s*. Edited by Noel Daniel. New York: Taschen, 238.

Jenkins, Greg. 2011. Phantom Clowns comment reply posted at PsiResearcher blog. May 3. Available at http://psiresearcher.wordpress.com/2011/04/11/280/.

Juno, Andrea, and Vicki Vale. 1987. *Pranks!* San Francisco: Re/Search.

KernGoldenEmpire.com. 2014. "A Small Town, a Photo Project, and the Nationwide Myth of 'Creepy Clowns.'" October 14. Available at http://www.kerngoldenempire.com/story/d/story/a-small-town-a-photo-project-and-the-nationwide-my/23530/e7kjzhz_9Eignb2Iwm4F5w.

King, Stephen. 2005. Stephen King interview about clowns. *Late Night with Conan O'Brien*. Episode 2119, September 23. Available at https://www.youtube.com/watch?v=P61KghCuQcU.

———. 2013. "The King of Horror in Hamburg, 20th of November 2013." Stephen

King on Pennywise, Carrie and Shining. Available at https://www.youtube. com/watch?v=smVMFNuGw2w#t=298.

Klein, Naomi. 1999. *No Logo: Taking Aim at the Brand Bullies*. New York: Picador Press.

Koller, Donna, and Camilla Gryski. 2008. "The Life Threatened Child and the Life Enhancing Clown: Towards a Model of Therapeutic Clowning." *Evidence Based Complementary and Alternative Medicine* 5, no. 1 (March): 17–25.

Kolozsy, Lee. 2003. "Rage in the Cage." Available at http://www.sideshowworld. com/13-TGOD/L-K/5-Rage/Tgod-LK-rage-in-the-cage.html.

Kupperberg, Alan, and Jon B. Cooke. 2007. Interview, transcribed by Brian K. Morris. *Comic Book Artist*, no. 16. Available at http://www.alankupperberg.com/ comicbook.html.

Kuruvilla, Carol. 2014. "Staten Island Clown Who Terrorized Borough Residents Unmasked." *New York Daily News*. March 28. Available at http://www.nydaily news.com/new-york/staten-island-clown-terrorized-borough-residents- unmasked-article-1.1737891.

Lacitis, Erik. 1991. "Alas, Clown Credibility Damaged by These Unflattering Stories." *Seattle Times*. June 25. Available at http://community.seattletimes. nwsource.com/archive/?date=19910625&slug=1291027.

Lasn, Kalle. 1999. *Culture Jam: How to Reverse America's Suicidal Consumer Binge— And Why We Must*. New York: HarperCollins.

LeDuff, Charlie. 2005. *Work and Other Sins: Life in New York City and Thereabouts*. New York: Penguin Books.

Levack, Brian. 2005. *The Witch-Hunt in Early Modern Europe*. 3rd ed. Harlow, UK: Pearson Education.

Lindfors, Bernth. 2014. *Early African Entertainments Abroad: From the Hottentot Venus to Africa's First Olympians*. Madison: University of Wisconsin Press.

Mannix, Daniel. 1976. *Freaks: We Who Are Not As Others*. San Francisco: Re/Search.

Marikar, Sheila. 2012. "Was James Holmes, Suspected Aurora Shooter, Inspired by Batman?" July 20. Available at http://abcnews.go.com/Entertainment/ james-holmes-suspected-aurora-shooter-inspired-batman/story?id=16822504.

Matthews, Washington. 1994. *Navaho Legends*. Salt Lake City: University of Utah Press.

McRobbie, Linda Rodriguez. 2013a. "Are Punch and Judy Shows Finally Outdated?" *Smithsonian*. February 4. Also available at http://www.smithsonian mag.com/arts-culture/are-punch-and-judy-shows-finally-outdated-10599519/ #2ZgmUcJ2FqsrpXqx.99.

———. 2013b. "The History and Psychology of Clowns Being Scary." *Smithsonian*.

July 31. Available at http://www.smithsonianmag.com/arts-culture/the-history-and-psychology-of-clowns-being-scary-20394516.

Mikkelson, David. 2007. "Citizens against Breast-Feeding." Snopes Urban Legends reference page. October 29. Available at http://www.snopes.com/inboxer/hoaxes/breastfeeding.asp.

Miller, John. 2012. *Face the Nation*. CBS News. August 12. Available at https://www.youtube.com/watch?v=czLIXiImb28.

Miller Van Blerkom, Linda. 1995. "Clown Doctors: Shaman Healers of Western Medicine." *Medical Anthropology Quarterly* 9, no. 4: 462–75.

Mintzer, Rich. 2010. *Howard Stern: A Biography*. Westport, CT: Greenwood Press.

Mitchell, Michael. 2007. "Details of Investigation Report." US Immigration and Customs Enforcement, Office of Investigations. Department of Homeland Security. October 9. Available at http://www.thesmokinggun.com/documents/revolting/christian-clown-perv-bust.

Moreton, Cole. 2000. "Attack of the Killer Clowns." *Independent*. October 8. Available at http://www.independent.co.uk/travel/americas/attack-of-the-killer-clowns-633827.html.

Morgan, Hal, and Kerry Tucker. 1984. *Rumor!* New York: Penguin.

Morlan, Kinsee. 2011. "Why (Not) Clown Porn?" *San Diego City Beat*. February 9. Available at http://www.sdcitybeat.com/sandiego/article-8725-why-(not)-clown-porn.html.

MTV. 2009. "He's Got the Whole World Wearing Clocks [1994]." March 13. Available at http://www.mtv.com/videos/misc/354305/hes-got-the-whole-world-wearing-clocks-1994.jhtml.

Murray, Rheana. 2014. "Sightings of Armed Clowns Continue to Spook California Residents." October 14. ABC News.com, available at http://abcnews.go.com/US/sightings-armed-clowns-spook-continue-californian-residents/story?id=26186819.

National Gang Intelligence Center. 2011. *National Gang Threat Assessment 2011: Emerging Trends*. Washington, DC: Federal Bureau of Investigation.

Ohlheiser, Abby. 2014. "Insane Clown Posse Loses FBI lawsuit; Juggalos a 'Gang.'" *TheWire.com* July 8. Available at http://www.thewire.com/national/2014/07/insane-clown-posse-loses-fbi-lawsuit-juggalos-a-gang/374093/.

Ornitz, Jill. 2014. "Jerad Miller: 5 Fast Facts You Need to Know." *The Heavy*. June 9. Available at http://heavy.com/news/2014/06/jerad-amanda-miller-las-vegas-police-shooting/.

Ouchy the Clown. 2008. Interview by the author. July 18.

———. 2014. Website at http://www.ouchytheclown.com/prodom.shtml.

Parsons, Zack. 2005. *Clown Porn*. Film review. Somethingawful.com. May 19. Available at http://www.somethingawful.com/horrors-of-porn/clown-porn/.

Phillips, Whitney. 2015. *This Is Why We Can't Have Nice Things: Mapping the Relationship Between Online Trolling and Mainstream Culture*. Cambridge, MA: Massachusetts Institute of Technology.

Pilgrim, David. 2007. "African Dip Carnival Game." February 1. Question of the Month. Available at http://www.ferris.edu/news/jimcrow/question/feb07.htm.

Prieboy, Andy. 2014. Interview by the author, September 14.

Radford, Benjamin. 2003. *Media Mythmakers: How Journalists, Activists, and Advertisers Mislead Us*. Amherst, NY: Prometheus Books.

———. 2013a. "Is the Creepy Staten Island Clown a Publicity Stunt?" LiveScience. com. March 26. Available at http://www.livescience.com/44383-staten-island-clown.html.

———. 2013b. "Scary Clown Terrorizes British Town." LiveScience.com. September 18. Available at http://www.livescience.com/39732-northampton-clown-terrorizes-town.html.

———. 2014. "Scary Clowns Plague California Towns." *Discovery News*. October 15. Available at http://news.discovery.com/human/psychology/scary-clowns-plague-california-towns-141015.htm.

———. 2015a. "Creepy Clown Sighting Surfaces in Chicago Cemetery." *Discovery News*. July 27. Available at http://news.discovery.com/human/psychology/creepy-clown-sighting-surfaces-in-chicago-cemetery-150727.htm.

———. 2015b. "Creepy Clowns Reportedly Stalk UK Children." *Discovery News*. October 19. Available at http://news.discovery.com/history/us-history/creepy-clowns-reportedly-stalk-uk-children-151019.htm.

Rittner, Ken. 2014. "Police: Cop Killers Heavily Armed, Wore Diapers." June 23. Associated Press in *Santa Fe New Mexican,* available at http://www.santafe newmexican.com/news/local_news/police-cop-killers-heavily-armed-wore-diapers/article_d253b223-da4d-5079-9cea-c07168b2cd52.html.

Ronson, Jon. 2010. "Insane Clown Posse: And God Created Controversy." *Guardian*. October 8. Available at http://www.theguardian.com/music/2010/oct/09/insane-clown-posse-christians-god.

Ross, Gene. 2002. "On the Set of *Ass Clowns 3*: One John's Undercover Glimpse into the Twisted World of Thomas Zupko." GeneRossExtreme.com. April 15. Available at https://web.archive.org/web/20021017171128/http://www.generos-sextreme.com/archives/dailys/41502.html.

Rotella, Carlo. 2004. "Un Clown Biologique." *American Scholar* 74, no. 4: 50–56.

Royce, Anya Peterson. 1998. "Commedia dell'arte." In *Encyclopedia of Folklore and*

Literature, edited by Mary Ellen Brown and Bruce A. Rosenberg. Santa Barbara, CA: ABC-CLIO.

Rushton, Bruce. 2013. "Death in the Jail." *Illinois Times*. October 10. Available at http://illinoistimes.com/article-12935-death-in-the-jail.html.

Scary Clowns. 2006. Kansas City, MO: Andrews McMeel.

Scheffler, Mark. 2003. "Scare Tactics: Why are Liberian Soldiers Wearing Fright Wigs?" Slate.com. August 1. Available at http://www.slate.com/articles/news_and_politics/the_gist/2003/08/scare_tactics.html.

Schoettler, Jim. 2004. "Clown Arrested in Child Porn Inquiry." *Times-Union* (Jacksonville, FL). May 26. Available at http://jacksonville.com/tu-online/stories/052604/met_15701133.shtml.

Scoles, Steve. 2013. "Video: Is This the Northampton Clown?" *Northants Herald and Post* (Northampton, UK). September 16. Available at http://www.northampton-news-hp.co.uk/VIDEO-Northampton-Clown/story-21675105-detail/story.html.

Shaw, Alexis. 2013. "Gunman Dressed as Clown Kills Former Mexican Drug Lord." ABC News.com. October 20. Available at http://abcnews.go.com/International/gunman-dressed-clown-kills-mexican-drug-lord/story?id=20625859.

Shut Up Little Man LLC. 2008. "Shut Up, Little Man: The Audio Misadventures of Peter and Raymond." Available at http://shutuplittleman.com/index.php.

Sideshow Mike. 2009. "The Original Krusty the Clown Homepage." Available at http://www.silverbox.com/krusty/debate1.html.

Silver, Carole. 1999. *Strange and Secret Peoples: Fairies and Victorian Consciousness*. New York: Oxford University Press.

Simmons, David. 2010. Interview by the author, March 18.

Simpson, Connor. 2013. "Northampton Solves the Mystery of the Creepy Clown." October 16. *TheWire.com*. Available at http://www.thewire.com/global/2013/10/northampton-clown-unmasked/70609/.

SizeofLight. 2010. Blog post at www.UnsolvedMysteries.com. September 21. Available at http://www.davidicke.com/forum/archive/index.php/t-135312.html.

Smith, Lucinda. 1991. "Parents, Cops Quell False Rumors of 'Killer Clowns.'" *Montclair Times* (NJ). June 6. Cited in Brunvand 2001.

Spitzer, Peter. 2008. "Hospital Clowns—Modern-Day Court Jesters at Work." *Lancet* 368: 534.

State of Nebraska v. Scott A. Harrold. 1998. Court of Appeals Nebraska. October 27. Available at http://caselaw.findlaw.com/ne-court-of-appeals/1234866.html.

Steele, H. Thomas. 2004. *1000 Clowns More or Less: A Visual History of the American Clown*. Cologne, Germany: Taschen.

Stott, Andrew McConnell. 2012. "Clowns on the Verge of a Nervous Breakdown:

Dickens, Coulrophobia, and the Memoirs of Joseph Grimaldi." *Journal for Early Modern Cultural Studies* 12, no. 4: 3–25.

Taylor, Jerry. 1981. "Police Discount Reports of Clowns Bothering Kids." *Boston Globe*. May 9, 18.

Thompson, Nato, and Gregory Sholette, Eds. 2005. *The Interventionists: Users' Manual for the Creative Disruption of Everyday Life*. Cambridge, MA: MIT Press.

Timpone, Tony. 2006. Interview by the author. March 18.

Van De Winkel, Aurore. 2015. "Hostile Clowns in France: Rumors, Contemporary Legends, and Ostension at Halloween 2014." Presentation at the International Society for Contemporary Legend Research, 33rd Conference. May 28. San Antonio, Texas.

Vincent, Rickey. 1996. *Funk: The Music, the People, and the Rhythm of the One*. New York: St. Martin's Press, 309.

WABC. 2005. "Clown Sentenced After Assaulting a Man and Stealing his Bicycle." 7 Online.com. August 19. Also available at http://afspot.net/forum/topic/124995-clown-sentenced-after-assaulting-a-man-and-stealin/.

Warner, Marina. 2007. *Monsters of Our Own Making: The Peculiar Pleasures of Fear*. Lexington: University Press of Kentucky.

Watson, Margeaux. 2006. "Flavor Flav: Totally Cuckoo?" *Entertainment Weekly*. August 11, 39–42.

Weinberg, Tim. 2007. "Don't Send in the Clowns." *Fortean Times* 226. August, 34–41.

Weiss, Mitch. 1991. "Clown Pleads Guilty in Attempt to Kill Wife." Associated Press. May 15. Available at http://www.apnewsarchive.com/1991/Clown-Pleads-Guilty-in-Attempt-to-Kill-Wife/id-74884cb3b1b101dd4afoe164ee39f1c9.

Welsford, Enid. 1966. *The Fool: His Social and Literary History*. Gloucester, MA: Peter Smith.

Wolf, Buck. 2002. "When Clowns Go Bad." ABC News.com. May 21. Available at http://abcnews.go.com/Entertainment/WolfFiles/story?id=91615.

Womack, Sarah. 2007. "Children Are 'Scared of Hospital Clowns.'" *Telegraph*. December 26. Available at http://www.telegraph.co.uk/news/uknews/1573644/Children-are-scared-of-hospital-clowns.html.

Woodstock, Sarah. 2008. "The Anti-Porno Clown Movement (We're Not Kidding)." Urbanette.com. Available at http://www.urbanette.com/porno-clowns/.

Zeman, Joshua. 2014. *Killer Legends*. Documentary film distributed by Gravitas Ventures.

Index